THE FAMILY CONCERN SERIES

Y0-DXH-633

This book is part of the Victor FAMILY CONCERN SERIES, a multivolume library dealing with the major questions confronting Christian families today. Each book is accompanied by a Leader's Guide for group study and a Personal Involvement Workbook for individual enrichment. All are written in a readable practical style by qualified, practicing professionals. Authors of the series are:

Anthony Florio, Ph.D., premarriage, marriage, and family counselor, *Two to Get Ready* (premarital preparation);

Rex Johnson, assistant professor of Christian education, Talbot Seminary, active in pastoral counseling, *At Home with Sex* (sex education and marriage preparation in the family);

Harold Myra, publisher of *Christianity Today, Love Notes to Jeanette* (sexuality and fulfillment in marriage);

J. Allan Petersen, speaker at Family Affair Seminars, *Conquering Family Stress* (facing family crises);

Nancy Potts, marriage and family counselor, *Loneliness: Living Between the Times* (dealing with personal loneliness);

Wayne Rickerson, family pastor, Beaverton Christian Church, Beaverton, Oregon and director of Creative Home Teaching Seminars, *Family Fun and Togetherness* (family togetherness activities);

Barbara Sroka, served on research and writing committees with Chicago's Circle Church and is active with their single adults, *One Is a Whole Number* (singles and the church);

James Thomason, assistant pastor at Calvary Baptist Church, Detroit, *Common Sense about Your Family Dollars* (family finances);

Ted Ward, Ph.D., professor and director of Values Development Education program at Michigan State University, *Values Begin at Home* (value development in the family);

H. Norman Wright, assistant professor of psychology at Biola College and marriage, family, and child counselor, *The Family that Listens* (parent-child communication).

Consulting editor for the series is J. Allan Petersen, president of Family Concern Inc.

GUIDE TO CURRICULUM SUBJECTS

	Wright—Communication THE FAMILY THAT LISTENS	Ward—Values Development VALUES BEGIN AT HOME	Thomason—Finances COMMON SENSE ABOUT YOUR FAMILY DOLLARS	Sroka—Singleness ONE IS A WHOLE NUMBER	Rickerson—Fun & Togetherness FAMILY FUN AND TOGETHERNESS	Potts—Loneliness LONELINESS: LIVING BETWEEN THE TIMES	Petersen—Crises CONQUERING FAMILY STRESS	Myra—Intimacy in Marriage LOVE NOTES TO JEANETTE	Johnson—Sex Education AT HOME WITH SEX	Florio—Premarriage TWO TO GET READY
adolescent children	*	*					*		*	
birth control								*	*	*
child development	*	*			*				*	
child discipline	*	*								
child communication	*	*			*		*		*	
church-family		*		*		*				
dating				*					*	*
death						*	*			
divorce				*		*	*	*		
emotions	*			*		*	*	*		*
engagement						*	*	*	*	*
finances			*				*			
friendship				*		*	*			
goals			*	*		*				*
leisure					*	*	*			
loneliness				*		*				

Love Notes to Jeanette

Harold Myra

While this book is designed for the reader's personal enjoyment and profit, it is also intended for group study. A Leader's Guide with Victor Multiuse Transparency Masters (for visual aids) and a Personal Involvement Workbook are available from your local Christian bookstore or from the publisher at $2.95 each.

VICTOR BOOKS

a division of SP Publications, Inc., Wheaton, Illinois
Offices also in Fullerton, California • Whitby, Ontario, Canada • London, England

Scriptures are from the *New International Version* © 1978 by
The New York International Bible Society. Used by permission.

Recommended Dewey Decimal Classification: 261.83418
Suggested subject headings: MARRIAGE; DOMESTIC RELATIONS

Library of Congress Catalog Card Number: 79-64037
ISBN: 0-88207-638-8

VICTOR BOOKS
A division of SP Publications, Inc.
P.O. Box 1825 • Wheaton, Illinois 60187

CONTENTS

Foreword

I am excited about the potential of this unique book by Harold Myra, publisher of "CHRISTIANITY TODAY." He is a pioneer. Married couples have long needed more than admonitions to communicate in order to develop intimacy in marriage. We all need models—models of truth, personal transparency, and beauty.

"Love Notes to Jeanette" is such a model. More than a book to be read, it is an experience to be shared by husband and wife—a kind of Song of Solomon. It reveals all of the facets of an intimate marriage relationship—romance, communication, conflict—and with experiences and images understandable to today's people. It can be the catalyst for the renewal of marriage vitality for an individual couple, or studied together by couples within the church.

The Leader's Guide has been especially designed as a church-sponsored marrriage enrichment program for couples. The focus is on encouraging the growth of intimacy between husband and wife by responding to the Scriptures. I anticipate great things for couples who value their marriages enough to learn together in this practical way.

The Family Concern Series is an encyclopedia of practical family information prepared in response to the needs of contemporary families. It enables the church, with its built-in structures for education and enrichment, to meet these needs with a thorough and long-term plan. Pastors and church professionals will find in the books many valuable resources. They focus on the needs of singles, marrieds, parents, and the family.

God uses people more than books to change people and this series helps people work together on their family needs. Each book can be used in a group study for mutual learning, encouragement, and support.

A Leader's Guide provides 13 study plans for adults in Sunday Schools, seminars, workshops, conferences, and retreats—complete with learning activities and visual aids.

A Personal Involvement Workbook enables each individual to get maximum benefit from the study whether alone, as a couple, or in a group. Worksheets and activity instructions are included. The Guide to Curriculum Subjects works as an index to the most important topics and where they are mentioned in each book in the series. It is a road map that will help you find quickly the information you need.

A special word of thanks and appreciation goes to Norman Stolpe. As Family Concern's editorial director he served as series editor for this project. His vision and relationship with the various authors enabled the concept to take form in reality. His hard work brought this series from planning to completion.

Victor Books and Family Concern have shared this vision and have cooperatively developed this comprehensive family ministry resource for individuals and churches. I trust God will deeply enrich your life and family through it.

J. ALLAN PETERSEN
Family Concern, Wheaton, Illinois

Preface

You Call These *Love* Notes?

People from Family Concern and Victor Books sat with me over lunch when I shared my suggested title for this book: "Love Notes to Jeanette." Positive reactions came immediately, from all around the table. But then a voice asked, "You call these **love** notes?"

The inflection indicated an edge of disbelief. Much of the book is conflict; obviously, I am not always loving toward my wife. But yes, I do call these love notes because our commitment to each other is this: to be in a loving relationship through all the bumps and crunches; to care about each other even when we are expressing our own hurts and frustrations. David Augsburger wrote a fine little book on marriage called "The Love Fight." Later, another publisher issued the same book as "Caring Enough to Confront." Both titles capture the idea that mates who face their problems head-on and with full frankness show a love which platitudes and avoidance don't.

At our luncheon, there was another question: "Harold, how do you feel you come off to the readers?"

"Probably not very well," I responded. "But that's OK, because maybe it will help those who read the marriage books, but find their failures discouraging. Perhaps if they see Jeanette's and my struggles they'll find hope. We are hopeful! We are committed to each other. We care enough to confront, for we have anchored ourselves to scriptural principles that will make a long-term marriage feasible."

How had I gotten into this business of opening up my marriage in print? Not from a particular desire to share my thoughts beyond Jeanette herself.

I'd received a phone call from Family Concern asking if I would do a book exploring the subject of intimacy in marriage. And could I pattern it in free-style prose since people found this readable and interesting?

I told them I'd think about it . . . and after a month or so agreed to do the project. A main reason I did so was Jeanette's and my experiences of sharing with other couples. A number of discussions we had participated in had been frank and open, and constructive. Sometimes it had been in the context of a Bible study; once it was in a church's Marriage Enrichment weekend; other times with close friends who felt secure enough to share. In each case, we have been fortunate enough to interact at fairly deep levels within a construct of clear biblical principles and commitments. Through the interchange, we know we have been helped. We know the other couples also benefited.

Having someone share a problem similar to yours can turn on lights. Hearing solutions others reach can stimulate means of viewing one's own situation.

A friend commented after reading the manuscript, "I thought since I knew you and Jeanette, I'd be mostly looking for what I'd learn about both of you. But I didn't. I found myself constantly thinking through my own marriage."

We trust his experience will be typical. Our hope is that this book will extend some of the healthy dynamics we have shared among other committed couples.

We all bring our faults as well as strengths to a marriage. We all have to live with both in our mates. And, perhaps most difficult, we must bear our own defects.

Our pastor recently started a Sunday School class on marriage communication by describing himself as "an eminent part-time failure" in this area. He read a quote from Philip Yancey's book "After the Wedding" that compared living with a mate with walking through a minefield, and admitted he had stepped on a few mines. We all have. Judging by the divorce rate, too many explosions occur, with the shrapnel ripping into warm flesh and the wounds then festering. Too seldom does loving communication heal the gangrenous hurts.

Conflict in marriage is inevitable. In one sense, it is the ideal setting for the Christian: there is so often need for repentance, forgiveness, reconciliation. We are in a spiritual warfare. Those who do let Christ form their responses can find a higher joy than those who play psychological tricks to avoid the issues.

This is an ordinary book of ordinary experiences. Various chapters show different moods, and many of the events may be similar to your own. These are slices of life, a simple sharing of our lives. How does God view these ordinary days, these moments with the kids and these touches of wife and husband? God surely cares. A God-inspired story of love, the "Song of Solomon," deals realistically with both conflict and tenderness between man and wife.

At the end of each chapter you'll find included a section of Scripture. About a year ago, this thought struck me: it is not often we read the Bible with the question, "How does this apply to my relationship with my spouse?" Each part of Scripture has principles that apply to this closest human relationship. I've found it stimulating to read with that focus—how does this apply to Jeanette and me, and how should I treat her? Certainly these basic scriptural principles should apply to my wife at least as much as to my neighbor or my enemy!

When you reach the Scripture portions, please read slowly, looking for basic principles. Many of these portions are not specifically related to husband-wife, and principles you draw may not hit the same areas or applications as my mind found. But I tend to believe you'll find it a helpful exercise to read Scripture with this focus. Of course, I've selected only a small portion of the Bible selections which could apply.

One more suggestion: some have found it works well to read the free-style prose aloud in a small group, and then discuss the way persons respond to the material. These readings do not take long, and discussion of individual experiences and scriptural principles can naturally develop from them. Or you may wish to read them aloud to your mate and then discuss them.

Several have asked me, "Has Jeanette read this? What does she think about it?" implying she might be uncomfortable with the openness in print. I wondered a bit myself about her reactions. When the book was half done I had her read the rough drafts. Fortunately, she responded enthusiastically, but I knew all was well when I overheard her on the telephone describing them to a friend as "romantic." In fact, her comment on the phone was the seed-thought for the title. Is it possible romance is less dependent on pleasant, gown-garbed evenings than kindness at a greasy sink? Is it romantic to confront? To forgive? To be reconciled?

A word of caution. One of the disadvantages of a personal book like this is the danger of transferring too many specifics. Some may think: "Ah, that's exactly how our marriage should work. My husband needs to be like Harold," or "My wife needs to be like Jeanette." As I wrote the section on gratitude for Jeanette's many, many good qualities, I wondered if some male readers might think, "Yes, that sounds like the sort of woman I need. I think my only solution is to trade mine in for a model of that type."

Each human being, made in the image of God, has unique qualities. It's all in the viewpoint. How do you view your mate? The key is to see what we can build on, how we can be not only grateful to our mates, but also to express that gratitude. To share with a loving concern which telegraphs beyond the faults, "I love you. Even when I see you at your least desirable, I love you."

I invited Jeanette to do matching chapters for this book, but she didn't see this as her gift. However, she did agree to dialogue with me for one chapter. The principles we discuss there together have become very important to us. We know that as the future comes, we will change, our children will change, and we will have adjustments to make. But one thing will not shift—the scriptural principles which represent a deep motherlode of truth. We plan to dig into that more and more deeply as we face our future—together.

DEDICATION

For our parents
Bill and Marion Austin
and
John and Esther Myra
whose loving marriages
are still alive and well.

1
DIVORCE

"You know, it could happen to us,"
you said to me,
sitting in your favorite chair as we sipped coffee,
digesting the news of the latest couples splitting up.
"No matter how great we think we have it,
if all those people can break up,
it could happen to us.
We're humans like them.
It **is** possible."

I didn't answer for awhile.
We were both incredulous at the news.
Men and women of maturity
decades-long marriages
so many have exploded, one after another.
Almost every week, another set of names.
Not him! Not her!
They're too sensible, too solid.

"You're right," I finally admit.
We've never joked about divorce,
never brought it up as an option.
We declared total commitment to each other
and must reaffirm that always.
But maybe realizing it could happen to us

helps us make sure it won't.
Maybe it jars us into realizing how easily love dies,
how love uncultivated, uncared-for, withers.
If all these Christians could break up,
couldn't we?

How terrible to think of an argument
someday when one of us feels
the need for the ultimate weapon,
"Well, obviously, there's no sense staying together.
We're just hurting each other,
just keeping each other trapped."
Those are words mouthed in kitchens
and bedrooms of "mature" Christian homes.

What do we mean by commitment?
How do we keep our love alive?
How do we make love grow
from early blossoms to summer fruit?

Remember how our love began?
Years ago, I offered you my arm
that September night we first went out.
You reached for it
as we leaped a puddle together.
Then you walked just close enough
to show you liked it.
I glimpsed your face under the streetlight,
excitement splashing gently on it. . . .
No commitment—just beginnings.

My arm pulled you that January eve
tight beside me in the car.
Midnight. Time to leave.
"Good night" wasn't quite enough,
and our lips touched gently
in a kiss as light as angel cake.

"I like you," it said,
but nothing more.

November air had rough-scrubbed our faces.
As we wrestled playfully
in your parents' farmhouse,
that moment I knew
and stretched toward you,
held you firmly
and breathed into your hair,
"I
LOVE
YOU."

The words exploded around us.
They meant far more than "you're nice,"
"you're sexy," "you're lively and fun."
They meant commitment.

Your words came back to me
in firm, sure sounds:
"I love you too."
And our kiss of celebration
was no romp of senses
but the beginning of a new creation.

Yes, I chose you.
Out of all the lovely girls I knew,
I chose you.
How marvelous are the women of Planet Earth,
hair flaring in the wind
rich browns and golds
a thousand delicious shapes
girls who laugh saucily
girls who read Browning
girls who play sitars
girls who fix carburetors.

Of all those fascinating possibilities,
I chose you.
Decisively. Permanently.
Is that self-entrapment?
Was a commitment made in youth
to bind me a lifetime?
Ah, but it was as strong as birth,
a fresh creation,
soon to be a new flesh,
you and I as one.

We chose each other.
We created something new under the sun.
You to shape me
and I you,
like a Luther Burbank original.
We, our own new creation,
to produce fruit wholly unique,
UNIQUE IN THE UNIVERSE!

Then the wedding,
flying rice and honeymoon
days and nights together.
Two persons
as unalike as birch and cypress
had chosen each other.
The world of rainspray and wet grass,
of autumn frost and crackly leaves,
would touch a new phenomenon.
We were born. Celebration.

The heavens laughed
and the sands of earth
lay ready for the tender feet
of our newborn self.
Does time change all that?
Were we naive? Now, after we have

loved, argued, laughed, given birth,
what does it mean
when I hold you and say,
"I love you"?

Without the young-love ecstasy,
is it required rote
or reaffirmation of our new creation?

"I love you."
My temples don't pulse as I say it.
My body does not ache for coupling,
not as it did.
Yet the words carry more fact
than ever they did in courtship.
They embrace a million moments shared. . . .

Standing together
atop Cadillac Mountain
and aching to absorb the blue-white-green beauty. . . .
Or angrily expounding to each other in the kitchen
about our particular stupidities,
then sharing a kiss ten hours later. . . .
Or driving all night through Pennsylvania and Ohio,
you sleeping, head on my lap,
me sleeping, head on your lap. . . .
Or stopping at an oasis and wanting each other so
    much. . . .
Bonding moments, holding us together.

How easily those bonds could be tyrannical.
"You always forget . . ." "You never think . . ."
And bitter moments bite into their flesh
with binding ropes that tie them to the
time and place instead of to each other.

Yet bonds can be

a thousand multicolored strands
of sorrow, joy, embarrassment,
of anger, laughter shared
as we watch God maturing us,
as we gently tell each other
of our joys, our fears,
even of our fantasies.

Rope is rope.
Experiences are much the same:
crabby days,
laughing days,
boring days.
We'll go through them "in love,"
by commitment to each other,
sharing, forgiving,
not blaming, not hurting.
Yet when we do hurt,
we ask forgiveness,
so the ropes will bind us together.

For if they don't,
they'll wrap around our throats,
so that each struggle will tighten the noose,
and we'll have to reach for the knife to cut the bonds.

Unthinkable!
But so many couples we know reach for that knife,
and divorce their bonds of love.

"I love you."
It sounds trite—
but not if it's remembering
the thousands of strands
of loving each other when we don't feel lovely,
of holding each other,
of winking across a room,

of climbing a park trail together,
of eating peanut butter sandwiches beside the surf,
and of getting up in the morning
thousands of times, together,
and remembering what we created
the day we first said "I love you."
Something permanent
and growing
and alive.

DIVORCE

A gentle answer turns away wrath, but a harsh word stirs up anger. The tongue that brings healing is a tree of life, but a deceitful tongue crushes the spirit.—Proverbs 15:1, 4

Therefore, as God's chosen people, holy and dearly loved, clothe yourselves with compassion, kindness, humility, gentleness and patience. Bear with each other and forgive whatever grievances you may have against one another. Forgive as the Lord forgave you. And over all these virtues put on love, which binds them all together in perfect unity.

Let the peace of Christ rule in your hearts, since as members of one body you were called to peace. And be thankful. Let the word of Christ dwell in you richly as you teach and admonish one another with all wisdom, and as you sing psalms, hymns and spiritual songs with gratitude in your hearts to God. And whatever you do, whether in word or deed, do it all in the name of the Lord Jesus, giving thanks to God the Father through Him.

Wives, submit to your husbands, as is fitting in the Lord. Husbands, love your wives and do not be harsh with them.—Colossians 3:12-19

Do not lie to each other, since you have taken off your old self with its practices. . . .—Colossians 3:9

"It has been said, 'Anyone who divorces his wife must give her a certificate of divorce.' But I tell you that anyone who divorces his wife, except for marital unfaithfulness, causes her to commit adultery, and anyone who marries a woman so divorced commits adultery."—Matthew 5:31-32

Some Pharisees came to him to test him. They asked, "Is it lawful for a man to divorce his wife for any and every reason?"

"Haven't you read," He replied, "that at the beginning the Creator 'made them male and female,' and said, 'For this reason a man will leave his father and mother and be united to his wife, and the two will become one flesh'? So they are no longer two, but one. Therefore what God has joined together, let man not separate."—Matthew 19:3-6

As a prisoner for the Lord, then, I urge you to live a life worthy of the calling you have received. Be completely humble and gentle; be patient, bearing with one another in love. Make every effort to keep the unity of the Spirit through the bond of peace.—Ephesians 4:1-3

Do not let any unwholesome talk come out of your mouths, but only what is helpful for building others up according to their needs, that it may benefit those who listen. And do not grieve the Holy Spirit of God, with whom you were sealed for the day of redemption. Get rid of all bitterness, rage and anger, brawling and slander, along with every form of malice. Be kind and compassionate to one another, forgiving each other, just as in Christ God forgave you.—Ephesians 4:29-32

You, my brothers, were called to be free. But do not use your freedom to indulge the sinful nature; rather, serve one another in love.—Galatians 5:13

2

TEMPTED
TO
WANDER

Yes, I noticed her.
We both did,
and you looked over at me
with that little grin barely creasing your lips.

Her black hair contrasted with a light tan—
she was innocent, with a young, full figure,
a sexy walk and a saucy look that invited . . .
at least conversation—
and you knew
and I knew.

I like that about you.
No cover-ups.
You say, "Look at that gorgeous guy,"
and I grunt recognition,
and perhaps add a disparaging word.
You reveal your thoughts to me;
you relax with your reactions,
and through sharing them with me,
draw them to the circle of our love.

The momentary urge to flirt,
the adventure of testing one's own appeal,
enters and tantalizes any sexual being.

What do we do with this force
that sneaks into our thoughts and lures our eyes?
You and I,
we laugh with it,
aware of our bodies' reactions,
our brains' teasings,
and the emotions wither away,
or fuse into our passion for each other.
After all, if I weren't drawn to others,
would I have passion for you?
How normal all this is,
when we share our intimate thoughts.

But where does appreciation stop,
and lust begin?
Will we one day look at each other,
and yawn,
and desire someone else?

If I do not see beauty in you, my beloved,
it is because I do not nurture it,
because I let the light in your eyes fade.
You are lovely when you are beloved;
you reflect the pride and joy and sharing
which flows to you and through you.

Sam and Grace, though in their sixties,
are so in love that their whole life
is a dance
with each other.
They face the terrible moments together,
and laugh through the delights,
sharing all parts of life.
She is a beautiful woman,
made beautiful by her lover
who has spent a lifetime loving her.

Isn't that everyone's dream?
And yet so few find it.
Sexual lures anesthetize common sense
and weaken all that mutual trust,
all that healing flow of full communion—
Wandering eyes and thoughts so often turn
the dreams into a heinous sentence:
"I don't love you anymore."

The Beatles' phrase hangs in my mind:
"A love that should have lasted years . . ."
The little foxes enter in,
when my own pleasure dominates me,
when I dwell on what you owe me,
instead of how I can enrich your days
and give you pleasure.

I chose you once.
Can I conceive of your becoming
so unattractive to me,
that I could not offer you my love?
Could there come a time when I could not embrace you?
Some have become hardened,
even repulsed by their mates.
But cannot God's Spirit perform miracles,
even in this?
St. Francis embraced the leper,
because of God's Spirit
who filled him with love,
though the leper repulsed Francis.

We can only praise God for the gift He has given us.
Though our passions now rumble more quietly,
our love has many new dimensions
which embrace all we've shared—
childbirth and broken arms and job crises,

and listening to details of good and bad days,
and figuring out why we run the way we do!

We'll still wake up some mornings
grouchy and bad-breathed from the flu,
unappealing and irritable.
We'll face temptations:
I'll walk into some auditorium
and see a girl, soft and natty-slim,
smiling at me like the sun is rising.
She may incite those elemental urges,
the same ones you touched years ago,
when we first walked by Lake Michigan.

I'm a biological creature;
how easily the immature part of me could think,
"Rekindle the youthful flame!
Here is the germinal seed,
the life-force that leads to love,
adventure, zest,
Next to this,
the bed at home is a bore."

How childish! How like our little Gregory,
dropping one toy to grab another.
When you become a plaything
instead of my beloved person—
half of me,
my guts, my vitals—
then I discard everything of value.

Paul Tournier says he's known couples
who have achieved a "total communion,
only to lose it later on."
It's so easy to forget
that if we don't work in a thousand ways at our love,
if I don't make you beautiful,

by letting you know you are,
the bond we have will turn tyrannical
and bind into our tender flesh
with biting bitterness.
We could be tempted by bright-colored toys
instead of mature delights,
like an alcoholic who once thrilled to Shakespeare,
but now sits dull-eyed before TV reruns.
Love is not regained by dissipation
nor by loving our pleasures more than each other.

The Bible says it:
"Be content with the wife of thy youth.
Let her breasts
satisfy thee at all times."

They do, Lover.
They do.

TEMPTED TO WANDER

My son, pay attention to my wisdom, listen well to my words of insight, that you may maintain discretion and your lips may preserve knowledge. For the lips of an adulteress drip honey, and her speech is smoother than oil; but in the end she is bitter as gall, sharp as a double-edged sword. Her feet go down to death; her steps lead straight to the grave. She gives no thought to the way of life; her paths are crooked, but she knows it not.

Now then, my sons, listen to me; do not turn aside from what I say. Keep to a path far from her, do not go near the door of her house, lest you give your best strength to others and your years to one who is cruel, lest strangers feast on your wealth and your toil enriches another man's house. At the end of your life you will groan, when your flesh and body are spent. You will say, "How I hated discipline! How my heart spurned correction! I would not obey my teachers or listen to my instructors. I have come to the brink of utter ruin in the midst of the whole assembly."

Drink water from your own cistern, running water from your own well. Should your springs overflow in the streets, your streams of water in the public squares? Let them be yours alone, never to be shared with strangers. May your fountain be blessesd, and may you rejoice in the wife of your youth. A loving doe, a graceful deer—may her breasts satisfy you always, may you ever be captivated by her love. Why be captivated, my son, by an adulteress? Why embrace the bosom of another man's wife?—Proverbs 5:1-20

The mouth of an adulteress is a deep pit; he who is under the Lord's wrath will fall into it.—Proverbs 22:14

Do not lust in your heart after her beauty or let her captivate you with her eyes, for the prostitute reduces you to a loaf of bread, and the adulteress preys upon your very life. Can a man scoop fire into his lap without his clothes being burned? Can a man walk on hot coals without his feet being scorched? So is he who sleeps with another man's wife; no one who touches her will go unpunished.—Proverbs 6:25-29

One evening David got up from his bed and walked around on the roof of the palace. From the roof he saw a woman bathing. The woman was very beautiful, and David sent someone to find out about her. The man said, "Isn't this Bathsheba, the daughter of Eliam and the wife of Uriah the Hittite?" Then David sent messengers to get her. She came to him, and he slept with her. (She had purified herself from her uncleanness.) Then she went back home. The woman conceived and sent word to David, saying, "I am pregnant."—2 Samuel 11:2-5

Like a bird that strays from its nest is a man who strays from his home.—Proverbs 27:8

The Lord is in His holy temple; the Lord is on His heavenly throne. He observes the sons of men; His eyes examine them.—Psalm 11:4

(A psalm of David. When the prophet Nathan came to him after David had committed adultery with Bathsheba.) Cleanse me with hyssop, and I will be clean; wash me, and I will be whiter than snow. Let me hear joy and gladness; let the bones You have crushed rejoice. Hide Your face from my sins and blot out all my iniquity.

Create in me a pure heart, O God, and renew a stead-

fast spirit within me. Do not cast me from Your presence
or take Your Holy Spirit from me. Restore to me the joy
of Your salvation and grant me a willing spirit, to sustain
me.—Psalm 51:7-12

Above all else, guard your heart, for it is the wellspring of
life. Put away perversity from your mouth; keep corrupt
talk far from your lips. Let your eyes look straight ahead,
fix your gaze directly before you. Make level paths for your
feet and take only ways that are firm. Do not swerve to the
right or the left; keep your foot from evil.—Proverbs
4:23-27

So I find this law at work: When I want to do good, evil is
right there with me. For in my inner being I delight in
God's law; but I see another law at work in the members
of my body, waging war against the law of my mind and
making me a prisoner of the law of sin at work within my
members. What a wretched man I am! Who will rescue me
from this body of death? Thanks be to God—through
Jesus Christ our Lord!—Romans 7:21-25

3
ANGER

As you yank open the garage door,
we face each other like cobra and mongoose.
"Okay, you tell me why you're mad!"
I say in clipped, terse tones.
"Then it's my turn!"
And you do.
And I do.

Now, two hours later at the office
I'm still angry, tired, stretched out,
I can't work effectively.
I have no inner reserves
to make the phone calls
that require iron guts and a quick brain.

You were right this morning.
Your demands were reasonable.
And so were mine.
Both of us are taking on too much.
I've had four lousy days
and too many things have gone very wrong.

Mentally, I can dissect my anger;
I can see your side too.
But it still fumes in me,

Unlovable.
I am that.
Perhaps we both are,
rather often.
But lovers speak their love
even when they hurt.

Thank you, Lover.

ANGER

But Jonah was greatly displeased and became angry.
—Jonah 4:1

Love is patient, love is kind. It does not envy, it does not
boast, it is not proud. It is not rude, it is not self-seeking,
it is not easily angered, it keeps no record of wrongs. Love
does not delight in evil but rejoices with the truth. It
always protects, always trusts, always hopes, always per-
severes.—1 Corinthians 13:4-7

In your anger do not sin: Do not let the sun go down while
you are still angry, and do not give the devil a foothold.
—Ephesians 4:26-27

If anyone considers himself religious and yet does not
keep a tight rein on his tongue, he deceives himself and
his religion is worthless.—James 1:26

Consider it pure joy, my brothers, whenever you face trials
of many kinds, because you know that the testing of your
faith develops perseverance. Perseverance must finish its
work so that you may be mature and complete, not lacking
anything. If any of you lacks wisdom, he should ask God,
who gives generously to all without finding fault, and it
will be given to him.—James 1:2-5

If we have been united with Him in His death, we will certainly also be united with Him in His resurrection. For we
know that our old self was crucified with Him so that the

body of sin might be rendered powerless, that we should no longer be slaves to sin.—Romans 6:5-6

My dear brothers, take note of this: Everyone should be quick to listen, slow to speak and slow to become angry, for man's anger does not bring about the righteous life that God desires.—James 1:19-20

It is to a man's honor to avoid strife, but every fool is quick to quarrel.—Proverbs 20:3

Do not say, "I'll pay you back for this wrong!" Wait for the Lord, and He will deliver you.—Proverbs 20:22

Better is open rebuke than hidden love. The kisses of an enemy may be profuse, but faithful are the wounds of a friend.—Proverbs 27:5-6

In your anger do not sin; when you are on your beds, search your hearts and be silent.—Psalm 4:4

Pleasant words are a honeycomb, sweet to the soul and healing to the bones.—Proverbs 16:24

Finally, all of you, live in harmony with one another; be sympathetic, love as brothers, be compassionate and humble. Do not repay evil with evil or insult with insult, but with blessing, because to this you were called so that you may inherit a blessing. For, whoever would love life and see good days must keep his tongue from evil and his lips from deceitful speech. He must turn from evil and do good; he must seek peace and pursue it.—1 Peter 3:8-11

A rebuke impresses a man of discernment more than a hundred lashes a fool.—Proverbs 17:10

Better a meal of vegetables where there is love than a

fattened calf with hatred. A hot-tempered man stirs up dissension, but a patient man calms a quarrel. A man finds joy in giving an apt reply—and how good is a timely word!—Proverbs 15:17-18, 23

A patient man has great understanding, but a quick-tempered man displays folly.—Proverbs 14:29

4 CHILDREN

Intimacy!
With three kids scrapping?
Their ever-present voices?
Their calls for help?
If we're out of sight for ten minutes,
withdrawal pains alert their little brains,
and their voices cry out in summons.

Just this afternoon,
in a moment about as intimate as two can have,
our boy was suddenly banging,
pounding against the locked door
like a Great Dane,
incredulous at this blockage.

Remember the survey, Jeanette?
It must be ten years ago we read it.
It showed a "happiness" line for couples,
high on the chart before children,
but when children came
the line nose-dived;
when children left the nest
it started back up again!
Two adults, it appears,

can live with far less frustration
without a houseful of lively offspring.

What changes our own children brought
to our young, sane lives!
By the time we had two
(and one bathroom),
our kids had perfected a little system.
Since Daddy was not allowed out of sight,
if he entered the bathroom,
the child on duty
had thirty seconds or less to shout,
"Daddy! Quick!
Open the door!
I've got to go bad!"
The key word was bad, duly emphasized.
Somehow they had learned
we feared certain disastrous results.

What a change having children was,
from its being just the two of us!
Wall-to-wall toys throughout the basement.
The bitings:
    ("See the toothmarks on my arm!")
The competition:
    ("See my hideout, Mommy."
    "Well, look at mine!"
    "Mine's better!"
    "Well, mine's comfortable!")
Bathrooms with creative toothpaste smears everywhere;
clothes and shoes seeking every empty corner;
screams and wails of sibling conflict.

And yet there was caring.
When Michelle was pale and sick,
and was staying home from school,

she asked with great concern,
"Does Todd know the way to school?"

Remember the day
she forgot to meet him in school?
She was so upset,
sobbing to you,
"I forgot to get Todd!"
And when you found Todd,
and had him safe in the car,
she kept repeating,
"I am so stupid,
I am so stupid to forget you.
Aren't I, Todd?"
But he simply asked, "What?"
"Aren't I stupid to forget you?"
she asked again.
Ah, a chance for the sibling knife;
instead, a gentle response:
"No, you're not stupid, Michelle."

Life with children is one long series of intrusions.
It's like always being on nursery duty,
always a slave to their requests and needs.
A response is required for each new crisis.
Do the benefits outweigh
all this baggage in our lives?

We know our answer so very, very well.
We've shared so many incidents,
that even though "we" get interrupted,
these children bind us together.

Who but the two of us
will forever recollect five-year-old Todd
creating his own specialty "Dogwood Sandwich"—

three pieces of bread
two slices of cheese
two slices of bologna
lots of jelly
eaten with milk, fruit cocktail,
cookies, and anything else available.

And Michelle's rejoinder,
"I don't like bologna;
it gives me a headache."

Our children introduce tensions
but they relieve them too
with humor they don't understand.

Remember when I said to Michelle,
when she was only three,
"Do you know, Michelle,
that little girls are always asking
"Why? Why? Why?"
She responded, "How come?"

Or that same year,
saying grace at dinnertime:
"Thank you for making Mommy.
And Todd. And Daddy.
And thank you for factories
that make my babies."

Or the time my mother
told Michelle about Angora rabbits:
"They have beautiful wool—
white and long and fluffy."
Michelle added, "Sheep have wool too."
"Yes, but theirs is not as beautiful
as Angora rabbit wool."

"Oh," Michelle responded. "Well,
it wouldn't be nice to tell the sheep that!"

Each child's concerns, motions, mannerisms
touch us as with a magic wand.
You and I are more lovers
for these who have come from us.

Remember the day we sent Todd to bed
with no story
because he'd splashed all over the bathroom?
Great weeping and disappointment.
Then, as he walked down the hall,
I heard him declare,
"I'm mad!"
A minute later, I heard from his room,
"But I'm not very mad."
Seconds later, he said,
"Tomorrow I'll be happy.
I'm not very mad."

One of the most magical moments of all
was waking two-year-old Todd at midnight,
so he could see the Christmas tree.
Sleepy, wide-eyed,
he stood in pj'd awe,
delighted with the colored lights,
the spangled, sparkling tree.
We laughed quietly,
watching that unique roll of his eyes,
his touching the tree gingerly.
And then he ran to us
and hugged us.

Now, Greg is older
than Todd was that Christmas.

And we get the same little-boy delights.
Last week, I took him to a petting zoo.
Suddenly he asked,
"Do elephants ride bikes?"
"Uh . . . only in books," I answered.
"I ride tricycles, don't I!"
he declared with assurance.
"Yes, you do."
Then we turned around.
"Goodbye, elephant," he called loudly.
As we walked away,
Greg confided to me,
with considerable indignation,
"He didn't talk to me!"

Just yesterday, Greg came into the house,
crying, pointing to his leg.
"How did it happen?" I asked,
hugging him.
"The tree kicked me!"
"Oh?"
"And I kicked the tree!"

What do our children
contribute to our love?
Even the frustrations they add
draw us from our self-centered lives.

The awesome responsibility
of shaping three new persons in the world,
gives us—together—
a view of watching God at work,
in us, through us,
as our children trust us in His stead.

I remember once when Michelle was very small,
she was lying on the bed beside me.

Suddenly she rolled
and just launched herself into the air,
right off the edge of the bed.
It was only by providence
my arm was close enough
to reach out and grab her.
She was in the vicinity of her daddy,
and she absolutely trusted me.

Isn't this the same sort of trust
which must build year by year
between the two of us?

They trust us.
And we trust God
that the children He's given us
will help us grow in our love
and not cause it to sour.

Trust. Laughter. Sharing.
All bound up with our children.
Remember the breakfast when
Michelle was two?
We'd just finished pancakes and sausage
and leaned together
into a long breakfast kiss.
Suddenly, we were interrupted
by squeals of delight.
Michelle was grinning at us,
enjoying the sight of our embrace.
Then she ran to us
and landed roughly in our laps,
embracing and kissing us,
joining in with gusto.

How fitting,
how thoroughly appropriate

that our loving embraces
so often draw all three children
into one monkey-pile embrace
which has us all ending up
on the floor,
laughing.
How obviously healthy
that they squeal with delight
when they sense live, action love between us.
Their love has its roots in ours
as we share with each other.

How do we view the intrusions of children?
Yes, intimacy does get interrupted.
Talks we need get postponed.
And what dignity is there
for a father rushing for a pot
in times of the flu,
or a mother on her knees
scrubbing the latest mess?
Like all parents
we can "count the blessings,"
or we can allow the irritations,
the cramped freedoms,
the grousing at each other,
to cloud those blessings into the background.

There are moments when a child
meets our own needs
in ways we don't even realize.
The richness of watching God
work in young lives,
and work through us in them,
adds dimensions we would utterly miss
if it were just the two of us
staring into each other's eyes.

CHILDREN

When Jesus saw this, He was indignant. He said to them, "Let the little children come to Me, and do not hinder them, for the kingdom of God belongs to such as these. I tell you the truth, anyone who will not receive the kingdom of God like a little child will never enter it." And He took the children in His arms, put His hands on them and blessed them.—Mark 10:14-16

"Whoever welcomes one of these little children in my name welcomes Me; and whoever welcomes Me does not welcome Me but the One who sent Me."—Mark 9:37

From the lips of children and infants You have ordained praise.—Psalm 8:2a

Sons are a heritage from the Lord, children a reward from Him. Like arrows in the hands of a warrior are sons born in one's youth. Blessed is the man whose quiver is full of them.—Psalm 127:3-5a

The wolf will live with the lamb, the leopard will lie down with the goat, the calf and the lion and the yearling together; and a little child will lead them.—Isaiah 11:6

He who fears the Lord has a secure fortress, and for his children it will be a refuge. The fear of the Lord is a fountain of life.—Proverbs 14:26-27a

Many a man claims to have unfailing love, but a faithful

man who can find? The righteous man leads a blameless life; blessed are his children after him.—Proverbs 20:6-7

Dear friends, let us love one another, for love comes from God. Everyone who loves has been born of God and knows God. Whoever does not love does not know God, because God is love. This is how God showed His love among us: He sent His one and only Son into the world that we might live through Him. This is love: not that we loved God, but that He loved us and sent His Son as an atoning sacrifice for our sins. Dear friends, since God so loved us, we also ought to love one another.—1 John 4:7-11

I said to the Lord, "You are my Lord; apart from You I have no good thing."—Psalm 16:2

At that time the disciples came to Jesus and asked, "Who is the greatest in the kingdom of heaven?"

He called a little child and had him stand among them. And He said: "I tell you the truth, unless you change and become like little children, you will never enter the kingdom of heaven. Therefore, whoever humbles himself like this child is the greatest in the kingdom of heaven. And whoever welcomes a little child like this in My name welcomes Me."—Matthew 18:1-5

5
GRATI-
TUDE

You ruined my evening, Jeanette.
Instead of even a brief rest
(I was dragging),
you made us lurch like a herd,
all five of us, to McDonald's
and I never did get my project done.

Just because your day fell apart,
does that mean you should mess up mine?

Yes, my grievances are legitimate.
And yours?
Equally so.
You were wiped out
and the last thing you needed
was to make supper this evening.
But when you express your grievances,
I react.
I rise to my defense.
The cycle of just cause pitted against just cause—
isn't that the way the whole world works?
Is that the way to make a marriage work?

Contracts. That's the new idea.
Your jobs, my jobs,

and you'd better do them on time,
and do them the way the contract reads!
Pull your end of the load, wife,
give me what's mine
or face the consequences.
You express your grievance
and even though I don't have one at the moment,
my defense mechanisms will recall one,
my agile mind will leap from rock to rock,
to find your latest failing.
Like labor union and management,
we can charge and countercharge
for we are right!
My just demands are being trampled on.

Is that the way to make a marriage go?
Yes, it is—straight to a living hell.

Why do I want to cure you of your faults anyway?
Not because I love you, but rather
because they are inconvenient to me.
My complaints only increase your failures.
My grievances despoil your spirit.
It takes so many pieces
to make for a beautiful relationship.
Of course we don't love all the time.
Of course I fail. You fail.
So we can look at all the missing pieces,
make long lists of legitimate grievances,
and stare at those lists and seethe.

Oh, we need to confront sometimes.
And we do that well enough.
But even more, we need gratitude.
We can make lists of what we're grateful for.
We can change that normal reaction to attack
only through the healing climate of love.

A study done in a hospital showed that
gratitude was the most healing emotion of all.
When I think about things I'm grateful for,
healthy feelings flow.
But when I think of all I'm being cheated of,
I am ripped apart inside.

Short lists of grievances?
Long lists of things I'm grateful for?

I think I will make a list!
It could go on and on.
I'm grateful, Jeanette,
for the way you love our kids—
for the way you hug and tickle them,
getting all tangled up in a riotous "monkey pile,"
or grabbing little Gregory
and just squeezing the love into him.
Even when tears and shrieks
make bathtime a battle,
your love for them makes the warfare temporary
and always there's a forgiveness
and a gentle kiss and snuggle goodnight.

Remember when you read a book
and realized what marvelous strategy it is
to pay attention to kids when they're behaving,
not just when they're smearing the walls with shoe polish?
So you watched out the kitchen window,
ignoring a few minor skirmishes,
and when Michelle was gently pushing Todd on the swing,
you rushed out with your cookies and milk,
praising the brother and sister who love each other.

I'm grateful you listen to the kids
and find ways to light up their faces.
Remember the fish tank?

You spent hours at the store researching;
then you bought it
and gamely started reading diagrams
and screwing little pieces together,
and going back to the store for more instructions
and more instructions,
until you felt like dangling the salesman in the tank,
and then you washed the sand and got the fish,
and Todd's birthday present became the eighth wonder of
    the world,
with all three kids rapt for days
in front of their wriggling eel and snail and tigerbar.

It took a lot of energy and caring
and commitment to pull slimy, dead eels and swordfish
    out
and flush them down the toilet
and keep wiping off fingerprints,
but you love our kids enough.

I'm grateful for all the good ideas you unearth,
then try out on all of us:
new recipes, excursions, decorations.
You have zest that sometimes wears me out!

I'm grateful for who you are—
that your parents loved you and each other,
so that you could repeat that pattern
and joyously give yourself to me.
Remember picking out a soft peignoir set,
at Marshall Field,
for our honeymoon?
Remember the days before Michelle was born,
when you'd show me magazine shots of pregnant
    women—
lovely, soft-apparalled young matrons
with wistful glows from their fruitful bodies?

"Aren't they beautiful!" you declared,
and before long you had me believing
that women heavy with child were especially lovely crea-
    tures,
softly clothed in hanging finery.
I love the way you love to be pregnant
and love the birth itself,
taking part in the adventure
as if we were still in Eden,
birthing under the smile of God,
and joyously embracing the delights He gives.

I'm grateful you'll not only take charge
of baby-sitters
and your own car
and social engineering,
but also an intimate weekend in Chicago,
for just the two of us.

Remember that magic day
when we chose your engagement ring?
We pushed between walls of people,
through little shops and department stores,
trying to find the one.
Behind steel-webbed doors,
a stonecutter plucked a stone with his tweezers,
then carefully placed the diamond in your palm,
and your face said, Yes.

Then we sat in a steakhouse,
and your fingers squeezed my arm
as you said, very simply, "Thank you."
Somehow it seemed unnecessary—surprising—
a little gesture, but very, very nice.

And that night the two of us
walked in the middle of a quiet street.

It was almost midnight,
and the rain had just passed on to the next town,
leaving big drops on the overhanging trees,
which splattered down one by one.
The streetlights were giant fireflies
gauzed up in the mist
with a few wide rays escaping—
so thick I felt I could grab them.
Our feet were soggy
but I felt thankful for the rain
and for God
and for you.
I was thankful you were like sunshine—
in fact, people called you Little Miss Sunshine.
I was thankful for the way you thanked me
for little things,
for your attitude toward life—
the way you touched the grass
and talked about your friends
and grabbed my fingers in the city.

Can we still taste some of the engagement-days' magic?
Gratitude will help keep our love young
this year,
next year.
How easy it would be to make lists—
detailed lists—
of all the ways we disappoint each other.
Somehow, it's more natural to peer at a mate's failings
than at what we have and appreciate.
People would much rather stare at the hole
and gripe
than look at the donut that's there.
In fact, I criticize you
more than you do me,
and I'm grateful you don't harbor resentment.

"Whatsoever things are lovely . . .
and of good report,
think on these things."

Let's do that for each other, Love,
for then we do it for ourselves.

GRATITUDE

I thank my God every time I remember you. In all my prayers for all of you, I always pray with joy because of your partnership in the Gospel from the first day until now, being confident of this, that He who began a good work in you will carry it on to completion until the day of Christ Jesus.—Philippians 1:3-6

Your wife will be like a fruitful vine within your house; your sons will be like olive shoots around your table. Thus is the man blessed who fears the Lord.—Psalm 128:3-4

Those who live according to the sinful nature have their minds set on what that nature desires; but those who live in accordance with the Spirit have their minds set on what the Spirit desires. The mind of sinful man is death, but the mind controlled by the Spirit is life and peace, because the sinful mind is hostile to God. It does not submit to God's law, nor can it do so. Those controlled by the sinful nature cannot please God.

You, however, are controlled not by the sinful nature but by the Spirit, if the Spirit of God lives in you. And if anyone does not have the Spirit of Christ, he does not belong to Christ. But if Christ is in you, your body is dead because of sin, yet your spirit is alive because of righteousness. And if the Spirit of Him who raised Jesus from the dead is living in you, He who raised Christ from the dead will also give life to your mortal bodies through His Spirit, who lives in you.

Therefore, brothers, we have an obligation—but it is

not to the sinful nature, to live according to it.—Romans 8:5-12

An anxious heart weighs a man down, but a kind word cheers him up.—Proverbs 12:25

We always thank God, the Father of our Lord Jesus Christ, when we pray for you.—Colossians 1:3

For this reason, since the day we heard about you, we have not stopped praying for you and asking God to fill you with the knowledge of His will through all spiritual wisdom and understanding. And we pray this in order that you may live a life worthy of the Lord and may please Him in every way; bearing fruit in every good work, growing in the knowledge of God, being strengthened with all power according to His glorious might so that you may have great endurance and patience, and joyfully giving thanks to the Father, who has qualified you to share in the inheritance of the saints in the kingdom of light. For He has rescued us from the dominion of darkness and brought us into the kingdom of the Son He loves.—Colossians 1:9-13

Let the peace of Christ rule in your hearts, since as members of one body you were called to peace. And be thankful. Let the word of Christ dwell in you richly as you teach and admonish one another with all wisdom, and as you sing psalms, hymns and spiritual songs with gratitude in your hearts to God. And whatever you do, whether in word or deed, do it all in the name of the Lord Jesus, giving thanks to God the Father through Him.—Colossians 3:15-17

Devote yourselves to prayer, being watchful and thankful.—Colossians 4:2

A wife of noble character who can find? She is worth far

more than rubies. Her husband has full confidence in her and lacks nothing of value. She brings him good, not harm, all the days of her life. She is clothed with strength and dignity; she can laugh at the days to come. She speaks with wisdom, and faithful instruction is on her tongue. She watches over the affairs of her household and does not eat the bread of idleness. Her children arise and call her blessed; her husband also, and he praises her. Charm is deceptive, and beauty is fleeting; but a woman who fears the Lord is to be praised.—Proverbs 31:10-12, 25-28, 30

6
INDEPEN-
DENCE

We lie in the bed together,
backs of our heads on pillows,
resting easy.
But something troubles you.

"You don't need me,"
you say into the air and at me.
"You don't need me like I need you."
I turn my head toward you, and you add,
"You'd get along fine without me.
Wouldn't you?"

My brain reaches out to guide my tongue,
carefully, carefully,
as it would guide gently probing feet
in the dark near a ditch.
Honesty first, but love.
Above all, love.
Reach out to your mate
but tell the truth.

"Yes. I'd get along.
I'd be fine."

Don't give flip explanations now, tongue.

Just say,
"But I'd miss so much.
All your enthusiasm and sparkle.
You pry me out of my crustacean bed;
you throw off the stuffy covers."

"But I couldn't do without you,"
is your response.
"You don't need me—
not like I do you."

Your words don't accuse
but they carry a disturbing weight.
They are objective words
yet intoned with sadness, wistfulness
—and perhaps a longing?

I must confess to a certain pleasure at this talk.
Yes, I am self-sufficient.
I can do very well in this world, thank you.
I have drive, initiative, marketable skills.
Yes, if you died, I would weep
but I'd survive,
though the empty space would be there.

Yet even as I feel this,
another voice says,
"Your strength is good.
Yes, you would survive
but you forget something.
Somehow your strength is your weakness;
somehow this conflict is elemental,
a male-female incongruence,
a role tension in which you, as a man, can either exploit
or share the bonds,
the mutual weaknesses,
and thereby know a far greater strength."

I move toward you,
and my arm reaches around to your back,
my fingers kneading your neck muscles.
Gently, I fondle your hair.
My touch says "I love you."
But I don't have words beyond that.

Like a young tree in a choice garden,
I was given years of gentle pruning,
with soft earth around my roots,
gentle rain, and space and nutrients.
And now the tree stands strong
in a choice place in a lovely garden,
while so many in the forest are gnarled and twisted,
starved and crowded from the light.
And you too were raised in such a garden,
and you too are strong.

But we are not trees,
one standing proudly by another,
roots barely touching.
We are male and female
intertwined.
We are creatures who dance
in and out
in and out of each other's lives.
"And her desire shall be toward her husband,"
God said.
Are you more linked to me in your weakness
than I to you?

Yes, you gave up your life as an RN
to build our nest,
You suckle the children
while I build my self-sufficiency in the world.
You realize your dependence,
and I perceive my self-sufficiency.

When you anger me,
I grasp my independence;
I raise my head
and set my teeth:
I have options—
I don't have to listen to all this.
I can stand alone,
go back to the office,
and you can wither or prosper, as you wish.
The whispers of Satan ooze into my ear,
whispers of my self-sufficiency
and your vulnerability;
whispers like a poisonous vapor
come to dull our music—
sulphurous whispers that stop the dance!

Was Christ self-sufficient?
Yes, thoroughly,
but He wouldn't make a move
without communing with the Father.
He was free
—to do the Father's bidding.
He was intertwined with the needs
—of disciples,
—of the city He wept over,
—of self-sufficient ones like me.
Was He trapped by all this?
Or was He free in the Father's will?

We are both trapped.
Our children, Todd, Michelle, and Greg,
are they not too great a burden?
We must die for them daily.
At midnight when an earache intrudes,
when frustrated cries hit our eardrums and nerves,
when chatter turns our private, adult picnic
into a raucous robin's nest.

We want to be free—
to hear the piano recital at the college,
to dine at Henrici's
and to simply talk uninterrupted.
Yet out of our little deaths to self
comes redemptive joy:
the running feet of a welcoming child,
the whispers of love in the night
from a child just starting to understand.

Do I need you?
No. As you do not need to die to self
and yet you do,
and I do,
for herein is life.

These are mysteries—
sacred and great mysteries,
this dying for each other,
as Christ died for us.
Yet this sacred mystery is as common
as a hand plunged into dishwater.

Independent? Do I stand alone?
Yes, I can draw myself upright,
and stand like a boulder above the sea.
I can pace the deck like a sea captain,
nostrils flared, surveying the elements,
coping, adjusting, winning!

But if I stand apart from you—
only drawing from you what I need,
shutting you off,
finding escapes
so I will not need to die daily,
I cut off the redemptive joy.
I block what our love could be.

I need you, and I need to give.
I need to be needed,
and when I reject that
and stand invincible and self-sufficient,
I move from God
and from your love
and from asking forgiveness
and from vulnerability.

Like a tree,
I cannot move my roots,
for yours are intertwined among them.
Let us both be strong in God,
yet weak enough to draw from each other.
We are not rocks.
We are not islands.
We are lovers
whom God has put together.

I need you, Jeanette.

INDEPENDENCE

I slept but my heart was awake. Listen! My lover is knocking: "Open to me, my sister, my darling, my dove, my flawless one. My head is drenched with dew, my hair with the dampness of the night." I have taken off my robe—must I put it on again? I have washed my feet—must I soil them again? My lover thrust his hand through the latch-opening; my heart began to pound for him. I arose to open for my lover, and my hands dripped with myrrh, my fingers with flowing myrrh, on the handles of the lock. I opened for my lover, but my lover had left; he was gone. My heart had gone out to him when he spoke. I looked for him but did not find him. I called him but he did not answer.—Song of Songs 5:2-6

In the Lord, however, woman is not independent of man, nor is man independent of woman. For as woman came from man, so also man is born of woman. But everything comes from God.—1 Corinthians 11:11-12

When pride comes, then comes disgrace, but with humility comes wisdom.—Proverbs 11:2

A man's pride brings him low, but a man of lowly spirit gains honor.—Proverbs 29:23

Live in harmony with one another. Do not be proud, but willing to associate with people of low position. Do not be conceited.—Romans 12:16

Do not think of yourself more highly than you ought, but

rather think of yourself with sober judgment, in accordance with the measure of faith God has given you. Just as each of us has one body with many members, and these members do not all have the same function, so in Christ we who are many form one body, and each member belongs to all the others.—Romans 12:3b-5

Who is wise and understanding among you? Let him show it by his good life, by deeds done in the humility that comes from wisdom. But if you harbor bitter envy and selfish ambition in your hearts, do not boast about it or deny the truth. Such "wisdom" does not come down from heaven but is earthly, unspiritual, of the devil.

But the wisdom that comes from heaven is first of all pure: then peace loving, considerate, submissive, full of mercy and good fruit, impartial and sincere. Peacemakers who sow in peace raise a harvest of righteousness.— James 3:13, 15, 17-18

Carry each other's burdens, and in this way you will fulfill the law of Christ. If anyone thinks he is something when he is nothing, he deceives himself. Each one should test his own actions. Then he can take pride in himself, without comparing himself to somebody else, for each one should carry his own load.—Galatians 6:2-5

Speak to one another with psalms, hymns, and spiritual songs. Sing and make music in your heart to the Lord, always giving thanks to God the Father for everything, in the name of our Lord Jesus Christ.

Submit to one another out of reverence for Christ.— Ephesians 5:19-21

All a man's ways seem right to him, but the Lord weighs the heart. To do what is right and just is more acceptable to the Lord than sacrifice.—Proverbs 21:2-3

To man belong the plans of the heart, but from the Lord comes the reply of the tongue. All a man's ways seem innocent to him, but motives are weighed by the Lord. Pride goes before destruction, a haughty spirit before a fall.
—Proverbs 16:1-2, 18

7
INTER-
MISSION

This is the halfway point: time to stretch a little and digest the ideas.

The following dialogue represents a change of pace. Since so many readers suggested I include at least some of Jeanette's comments and interaction, she and I went off for a short weekend in Wisconsin and talked into our recorder. Then we edited the roughs into what follows.

This brief bit of conversation gives insight into the personality differences we must deal with, and a few thoughts about solutions. Other couples face different dynamics, different adjustments. Frankly, we would be disappointed if others took our marriage as a necessary model. There are basic biblical principles all of us must follow, but they are more like atoms and molecules than precut lumber. From molecules can come creations as diverse as hummingbirds, dolphins, and dogwood blossoms. Each marriage needs the freedom to become a unique creation.

The main point of this intermission may be that frank dialogue and vulnerability are important. They do not sabotage a relationship, but rather break down walls and encrustations which limit growth. This is not a definitive "model" discussion, but simply a small slice of our interaction.

Dialogue: Seeing from Both Sides

Harold: Let's start out on the topic of the first chapter: how do we commit ourselves? How do we avoid divorce and love each other forever? Let's get very practical.

Jeanette: One way is to seek out Christian friends who are as committed to their marriages as we are. Like the two other couples we shared with on vacation in the Ozarks. The six of us sat around the whole week talking about how we can make our marriages better. There was no major complaining about spouses except in a kind, questioning way—how we can change this or that behavior. All of us were so committed, it was an uplifting week.

Now if we had spent the week with couples who don't care about each other, I think that would have been a destructive week. It would have put little seed thoughts in the backs of our minds. Doubts seep in so subtly. We hear one more Christian leader is divorced and it eats away.

Harold: I agree. Yet it also jolts us out of apathy. It's helped us say, "This is serious. Before God we said our marriage is permanent, but it's only as permanent as we make it." Hearing about the divorces makes me feel ill, yet it also says to me, "You really have to make our relationship a priority!"

For instance, we can so easily take each other for granted. We treat our mates worse than strangers. Do you remember when we were in the car with Fred and Elaine? You asked Fred to hand you something. For some reason he thought it was Elaine talking and answered gruffly. His tone implied, "What's the matter, Dear? Don't you have your act together yet?" The fascinating thing was Elaine's response. She picked up that he didn't know he was speaking to you. She said, almost aghast, "Dear, that's Jeanette you're talking to!"

Obviously, Elaine was saying it was normal for Fred to talk like that to her, but not to you. Fred would never have used that tone on you! We talk to our spouses in ways we would never talk to someone else.

Jeanette: I've said so many things to you I would never say to someone else, like, "Hey, would you go brush your teeth: you've got bad breath."

Harold: Well, we should be able to share a problem like that without embarrassment. That's good. But what I'm referring to is the tone of voice that demeans, that says, "Hey, you jerk, aren't you done yet?" Or, "Are you bugging me again?" It's a lack of respect. I observed it carefully that entire weekend at the Ozarks. There wasn't real nastiness, but when there was a tone of disrespect, it was always toward a spouse.

Jeanette: Did you and I do it?

Harold: Some. We all did. The tone of voice between spouses is too often less respectful than the tone toward someone else.

Jeanette: Remember when we were walking through a honeymoon resort and I said, "You can tell the newlyweds immediately by the way they look with interest when the other person is talking"? Remember I said, "Let's make people think we're newlyweds by the way we look at each other and talk to each other!"

Harold: Wouldn't it be great if we could think consciously, "How am I talking to my spouse?" It would help us affirm each other. And that's not fake. That's not hypocrisy.

Jeanette: In a way it's fake at first if you're not used to it.

Harold: But it's like good manners. Why shouldn't you show good manners and politeness toward your wife? As C. S. Lewis said, one of the things about getting to be a good Christian is getting into the machinery of being a Christian. So you don't get anything out of going to church? So what. Go to church for a while and you might get something out of it. You don't get anything out of the Bible? Read it for a while. You'll eventually get something out of it. It's the same thing here. Get into a pattern of speaking with a loving tone of voice to your wife, and eventually it may become natural.

Jeanette: Respect—you have to have respect for your spouse! You and I do respect each other, but what about other couples? If they don't respect each other, then what? They can't fake it.

Harold: They have to find something they do respect.

Jeanette: Yes. And major on that.

Harold: There's no easy answer on that one. Some mates have problems that are very complex.

Jeanette: By the way, I don't respect the way you dress.

Harold: Yeah. OK.

Jeanette: What am I supposed to do about it? It does bother me.

Harold: It does bother you?

Jeanette: Yeah. That you're not real manicured and that you don't particularly care about clothes and styles. It does bother me, but what shall I do—repress it?

Harold: From my point of view I simply don't go to your extreme. I like the way you dress. That's fine. But to me you spend a lot of bucks. From my viewpoint, I'm right where I ought to be. I look at these trousers, for instance, that I have on. They're six years old and have those poly-ester snags. I could throw them away, but I'd feel guilty. They're not worn out. To me it's unethical to toss them.

Jeanette: And I am irritated that you wear trousers full of snags. In my way of thinking you don't care how important it is to me that you don't wear trashy clothes around.

Harold: But to me they're not trashy at all. They're just kind of half worn in, and to me it would be wrong to spend more money.

Jeanette: When I'm all dressed up and I've got my makeup on real nice and my hair is freshly washed, you sometimes comment, "Hey, you look nice." You like it when I look nice, and when you're dressed up ready to go to the office in your three piece suit and your shaving lotion on I say, "Oh boy, why don't you stay home for a while?"

Harold: Well, OK. I see that. I am dressed up a fair amount and I figure I'm dressed up all day every day and I ought to be able to bum around at night sometimes.

Jeanette: It's not exactly what you wear. Maybe it's the way you wear it, slouched in a chair.

Harold: OK. My fifth-grade teacher told me I'd always be slouchy.

Jeanette: I don't like slouchy posture.

Harold: So, I should work on that.

Jeanette: Oh, I hope not! Then I'd have to work on something I don't want to change. I mean, it's nice that these little things are all I don't like about you. I'm very fortunate that we can talk about it, that we're relaxed about it.

Harold: Yes. Neither of us gets upset. But what about the book? You've said you like it, but there must be some areas that make you a bit uncomfortable.

Jeanette: Well, I think I'd change that line from St. Francis about embracing a leper. I mean, am I that bad? When I've got bad breath, and no makeup, and my hair is a mess, is that as bad as hugging a leper?

Harold: I was thinking of the extremes when I wrote that. There comes a time when apparently some husbands just cannot stand the thought of their wives. Yet God tells us to love even our enemies. How in the world could I go so far from the point where I loved you to thinking you were repulsive to touch? Yet this happens all the time in marriages. And I'm saying, here was St. Francis, who did look at a person who was repulsive. In fact, the idea of getting close to a leper terrified him. But the love of Christ constrained him to get down off his horse and embrace that leper. What I was saying is, I can't conceive coming to that point where you'd be repulsive to me. Yet even if you were, that emotion can be broken through and changed by Christ's love—by seeing as He sees.

Jeanette: You know that feeling of repulsion can happen, because we've seen and we've heard other people say they couldn't even stand to be near their mates.

Harold: I doubt that will ever happen to us. But certainly there are times when we're neutral toward each other or even angry. But shouldn't I be constrained with the same thing St. Francis was? There's a legend that after St. Francis kissed the leper and the leper kissed him, St. Francis rode away from the leper, and looking back saw that the leper was really Jesus Christ. Legend, yes. But you are Christ to me in the sense that you are the awesome soul presented to my senses. "If you do it to the least of one of these, My brethren, you do it unto Me," Christ said. If I can't reach out to you, how am I showing the love of Christ? How does our love transcend the ordinary passionate love? How is Christian love different from "ordinary" love?

If the Bible says to love your enemy, what in the world must you do to your wife? Even if she is terribly difficult to live with. Even if she's in an irritable, angry mood. I'm not saying I always do that. But I'm saying that the lesson of St. Francis which changed his whole life should be a goal and a lesson for us.

Jeanette: But how does that relate to sexual love? Shouldn't you feel a desire for the body? Like you're saying, here we are, two people lying in bed together. At the moment we have no desire for each other's bodies. Doesn't that concern you sometimes?

Harold: Well, I think that's just normal. The level of intensity does not at all stay as high as it is on the honeymoon.

Jeanette: People would be pretty exhausted.

Harold: They'd do nothing but hop in bed together. The business of life is much broader. But I do think that if a couple is really loving each other verbally and in the vibes they give to each other throughout the day, that that leads ultimately to physical love.

Anything else you feel uncomfortable about in the book?

Jeanette: The accusations like, "I ruined your evening," and "I made us lurch like a herd to McDonald's." People reading it are going to say, "Yeah, what a creep she is. He had a hard day at the office." I want them to see my side of the story too.

Harold: Like?

Jeanette: Why did I need to get to McDonald's? I can't remember specifically. But say I was making telephone calls for my church committee half of the day. I'm drained from listening to people or asking favors. OK. It's not earthshaking, but I was doing what I felt was my responsibility. Maybe that day I went over to school as a volunteer in Michelle's classroom. The teacher needs volunteer help and I feel an obligation, so I go over there and spend half a day. Sure, it was enjoyable, but I didn't stay home and get the laundry folded and supper made. And then the kids came home, both with school friends, and I'm giving them snacks and talking nice to them and hugging them and making them feel good about themselves. And let's say I've just scrubbed the floor because we've got company coming for the weekend. I don't feel like having us get junk all over the kitchen floor because I'd like to keep it clean at least until tomorrow morning. So I want to go McDonald's.

But I don't know that a day ahead. I can't predict and say, "Hey, tomorrow I'm going to be beat, so take us to McDonald's." Instead I hit you with it on the spur of the moment. You weren't in the mood to go and I wasn't in the mood to fix supper.

Harold: Good point. Both of us like to be warned ahead, but it doesn't work that way.

Jeanette: Right. You didn't know a day ahead either— to say, "Hey, Jeanette, tomorrow when I get home from work don't hit me with any problems."

Harold: We both start the evening with a whole day's worth of tensions, and sometimes we don't have the energy to get through the evening in good spirits.

Jeanette: A crisis is worse when we're unprepared for it. But these things can't be planned ahead.

Harold: We both want to do too much. We're over-committed. There just isn't the energy level to get it all done. I love the way you work with our kids. I think it's great you're active in church. We have to accept each other for the strengths and weaknesses that we have.

Jeanette: Even if I spend my afternoons running here and there and don't have supper ready when you get home?

Harold: Well, isn't everything balanced? You think it's great that I work hard in the office. You don't want me to be so wrapped up in that that I don't have any energy at night. Both of us think what the other does is great, but—

Jeanette: Each of us wants the other to be a superperson!

Harold: That is the thing. For us to perform for each other, to enrich each other, we have to be superpeople. And when the other doesn't quite perform up to expectations we think, "Hey, what's your problem?"

Jeanette: Yet you perform well for me because usually you do things with the children. You help me tuck them in at night, and listen to them, and bounce them around, and touch them a lot. You tell them how great they are and listen to them tell about school. You perform well as a husband because you listen to me, care about me. You encourage me. So I'm saying you're almost a superperson for me.

The only other thing I want out of you is I want you to think I am the superwoman for you! I want you to think I'm performing very well as a wife. I feel you disapprove of my lack of organization. So I feel guilty and then constantly try to tell you what a fantastic job I'm doing raising our children.

Harold: And you are.

Jeanette: Hmm. I keep trying to prove it to you.

Harold: And that's largely my fault. I don't feel judged by you. Perhaps there's less pressure on the man to measure up to the wife's expectations.

Jeanette: Yeah. I resent that to a degree. We've said everyone's got strengths and weaknesses. How come my weaknesses aren't acceptable and your weaknesses are acceptable? It's acceptable for a man not to want to go to McDonald's with his children, but it's not acceptable for a wife not to get the laundry folded. You get all your pats on the back for being a hard worker in the office, but where do I get my pats on the back?

Harold: That's a key factor—the wife is more dependent on the husband for emotional support. She feels a greater imperative to please him.

If we feel like failures in certain areas, then what are the solutions? You do need to get from me either an appreciation for what you're doing or a specific appraisal of what I believe can or should be changed.

Jeanette: Agreed. Actually I feel very good about myself and very good about my duties and roles—until I meet up with somebody who is my age or older and has a very challenging job. And in comparison, my job is just so easy.

Harold: You're threatened by other people? Shouldn't it come down to you and God deciding priorities?

Jeanette: Between me and God and between me and you, it's ok.

Harold: Then you shouldn't at all feel threatened by what other people—

Jeanette: I guess I have to explain why I do not have all these things done. I do have time to do them. I have to explain, "Oh well, I'm just not an organized person."

Harold: So you feel guilt. And this guilt, much of it comes from me? You feel I kind of, if not consciously, subconsciously judge you?

Jeanette: Certainly. Because you're better than I am. Because being organized is better than being unorganized.

Harold: Well, I guess I agree with that. But being enthusiastic, as enthusiastic as you are, is better than being unenthusiastic.

Jeanette: In a few people's eyes. But to many, my enthusiasm doesn't count for much.

Harold: So what? If you are really enthusiastic about your involvement with God and what God is telling you your ministries are, and if you don't feel guilt from Him, that's healthy. If you're only getting from others and from your husband a rejection of your personhood, that's our fault. You need to be accepted.

At the same time, we have to be honest about areas we want each other to change. You want me to shape up in certain areas too.

Jeanette: Yeah. Ten pounds worth.

Harold: Yeah. Really. What else?

Jeanette: Keep your fingernails short, pitch your tacky clothes, keep your teeth brushed and your breath sweet, at least as much as possible.

Harold: I guess we need this love thing. What's unimportant to us we should do for our mate anyway when we realize how important certain things are to our mates.

Jeanette: But all I'm asking you to do is cut your fingernails and lose ten pounds and keep your teeth brushed. You're asking me to get organized, be less spontaneous— to change my personality!

Harold: No, I don't think so. Let's face it, we've come a long way from when we first got married and we found out how different we were.

Jeanette: You mean I've come a long way.

Harold: No, we've both come a long way in that I have become pretty accepting of a much more relaxed lifestyle. You recall that I was far more compulsive—

Jeanette: So you've given in.

Harold: Well, you have come part way toward me and I

toward you. But I was much more compulsive before in saying, "Look, I want to eat exactly at six. I want such and such—"

Jeanette: And I've got a lot bigger house and three kids now and more responsibility.

Harold: Right. You've got a lot more to do.

Jeanette: Here's what I used to hate. You used to say, "From now on, I am going to get up at 7, eat at 7:15, leave at 7:25, be home at 5:20." I was so threatened by that because I couldn't bear the thought of being boxed in for the rest of my life to these time schedules. And I would get frustrated and angry because every month you'd change your 'from now on' speech. And one day I exploded and I said, "You never can make up your mind as to what schedule you're on!"

Now you say instead, "You know what I'd like to try for a while and see if this works? I'd like to try getting home at 5:20," and I relaxed. I thought, well, we'll work on it together and if it doesn't work out we'll change it.

You were literally going to the five minutes. You'd write down from 7:30 to 7:50 you were going to—

Harold: Well, that's the way I like to live. I am happiest when I am in control of my life. I might schedule an hour with the kids to just romp around, but I don't like to slide into every activity by happenstance. I don't want to just kind of slush through life, and at the end of a month feel, "Hey, where'd this month go? I never did get around to reading Tolstoy." If I don't schedule my life I won't do the things that are important to me.

Jeanette: That sounds very admirable, doesn't it? My slushing through life sounds pretty poor.

Harold: But you were just saying I'm rigid, down to the five minutes, implying you can't really live that way. Of course, if I'm giving you these vibes—

Jeanette: Like you said—slushing through life. That's what you said I'm doing, slushing through life.

Harold: No, I said I don't want to do that myself. I'm

fighting against my own tendencies. I don't care how you live your life because you're enjoying it. When I used the slushing-through-life phrase, I was saying I get frustrated at myself when I am not really in charge of my life. If I am putting a guilt trip on you, I don't mean it that way. That's what I want for me.

Jeanette: But, you also said that what I could do that would be most helpful to you would be to work with you on your schedules and to be—

Harold: Well, right. Not necessarily you doing the same thing that I'm doing, or whatever, but so that our schedules don't conflict.

Jeanette: But to have dinner ready at 6:35 every night and to have the house quiet so that you can read "Time" magazine every Tuesday between 7 and 9 . . .

Harold: Well, now I'm looking bad, as if you're being my servant . . .

Jeanette: It is your turn to look bad (wry smile).

Harold: OK. It's my turn to look bad. I'll buy that.

Jeanette: 'Cause I'm really a very lovable person (wrinkles nose in lovable manner).

Harold: Yeah. I'll buy that, too. And you're very cute when you stick your nose on mine and kind of wrinkle it around. But if I read "Time" magazine from 7 to 9 uninterrupted on let's say Tuesday night, then on Wednesday nights you should get from 7 to 9 to do what you want. Go to a church meeting, read "Redbook" magazine, or whatever.

Jeanette: You mean HARPER'S! Let's keep my image intellectual.

Harold: Of course! Actually you read "Psychology Today," "Time," "Esquire," and "Harper's."

Jeanette: What I like about you is that you are fair and you would let me go out to breakfast on Saturday morning.

Harold: Or go to a church meeting.

Jeanette: Church meetings sound so trite. People make fun of that. Like the other day when we were at lunch, I wanted to tell everybody that I'm on the Welcome Wagon board, I swim every day, that I'm a volunteer over at school, and then a little postscript, and I'm working on some church committees and teaching Sunday School and Junior church.

Harold: This is important, how people view your time?

Jeanette: Very much so.

Harold: Would you call that a spiritual problem or psychological?

Jeanette: The spiritual problem is how I handle it. It bothers me that I'm so concerned about my image. Partly it's because of these women's lib speeches. I am a happy, contented housewife. Why do I have to go around explaining to people that I'm happy?

Harold: Well, exactly. It's between you and God. Don't you feel "liberated" women sometimes make their speeches to feel OK about themselves too? And if there are fewer and fewer families with nonworking mothers, maybe you feel like one of a vanishing breed.

Jeanette: Which makes me more valuable.

Harold: Which makes you very valuable.

Jeanette: It almost always boils down to a spiritual thing—whether I'm contented with my life, whether I'm doing what the Lord wants me to do, and how He wants me to do it . . . with the right attitude. If I'm talking to the Lord about these church committee people I'm working with, I have compassion for them and the job is fulfilling. Otherwise I get irritated and it ruins my day.

Harold: When I go to the office or you go to the church committee, our attitude, our walking with God is the key. But as a couple how do we do that? How do we maintain that godly spirit, perspective, and attitude? I think we have to help each other. We have to really encourage each other.

For instance, I should ask you what really gets you turned on about the Lord. Church? Small prayer groups? You should ask the same of me, because I don't think they're the same for the two of us. I really enjoy going off and reading a good book by Tozer, but you would enjoy hearing a man like that speak. And we should pray together more.

Jeanette: Remember that your spiritual experiences were threatening to me for a while? When you sensed that, you just didn't share very many of your spiritual thoughts with me. You could see that I'd get too threatened because your thinking was much deeper than mine.

Harold: Well, let's say more abstract. I don't know about deeper.

Jeanette: We just have to get in the habit of praying together more. It can be awkward. I mean, if you're really honest, that is really the intimate sharing—praying together!

Harold: Right. Really admitting where you are. Confessing your weakness, your core thoughts. As you say, that's intimate.

Jeanette: There's no hiding.

Harold: How do you react to spiritual prodding?

Jeanette: There's a fine line between prodding and encouraging, between being pushed or gently led along, hand in hand. If I feel you share your struggles with me, not only your victories, then that helps me.

Harold: Yet if one mate really feels the other mate is failing spiritually, they feel frustrated that he or she is not enjoying a rich, spiritual life.

Jeanette: Then they need to very lovingly sit down and say, "I feel frustrated for you," rather than saying, "I wish you would go and spend some time reading the Bible."

Harold: In the husband-wife relationship, the "judge not" verse is more important, perhaps, than in any other relationship. As soon as one puts himself in the position of a judge, spiritual or otherwise, he starts that dynamic of "I'm right, you're wrong."

Jeanette: Yes. But it's so easy to judge because you know your spouse best. You know the failures. However, one thing that sort of surprises me is that you don't share very much of your spiritual victories. You share much more of your failings and your struggles. I don't relate to where you struggle. You're wrestling with concepts that don't bother me at all. I don't question the way God's running the world. I don't relate to your struggles, but I might be able to relate more to your good communications with the Lord.

Harold: I think there are two reasons. I don't like to come off like a spiritual braggart. The other is, I know I'm going to fail again. Maybe I've been praying on the Prairie Path and it's been great. But if I say, "I just really broke through to the Lord," it seems like I'm saying, Jeanette **you** ought to get out on the Prairie Path! You ought to get with your Bible! Also, I feel that maybe two days from now I'm going to have a real spiritual downer.

Jeanette: OK. I'm the same way. The other week I was telling you about all the little things I thank the Lord for. That's been going on for a long time, but I never tell you that stuff. I figure they're insignificant to anybody else. I know you don't pray like that. If I go out on a rainy day worrying the car might not start and I won't make my appointment, and the car starts right off the bat, I say, "O thanks, Lord, that the car started!" To a lot of people that seems silly.

You thank the Lord for helping you to understand some deep thing and my mind can't be bothered with that. So that's why we're not real comfortable sharing because we don't pray alike. But is it helpful for me to tell you that?

Harold: It's helpful for me to know how you're talking to the Lord. It's an encouragement. If I know you have an active, spiritual life, it helps me to have one.

We're different, yes. And my frustrations are different. But I basically have to thank the Lord for the same things you do. For health and food. And after all, it is the simple things in life that make all the difference—whether you have a bad digestion or avoid accidents. In many ways, we thank Him for the same things. Sometimes I think we accentuate our differences too much. It makes a good talking point, but basically we're very much the same.

Jeanette: You mean we use our differences as a cop-out? We use them as an excuse not to share spiritual things?

Harold: Yes. When you come right down to reading Ephesians, it's really not that much different for you or for me about obeying the Lord or reaching out to our neighbor, in our relationship to each other, and all the rest. We're different, but still, the spiritual life is the same essential struggle against carnality, and allowing God to take over.

Jeanette: We can pray for each other about some things without really understanding each other. I pray for you when I get scared about your struggles. I get worried, so I start praying for you. But I need you to pray for me, too! I need to show a lot of love to people that grate against me. And I need your prayers for me so that I will handle our children in the right way.

Speaking of children, do you think this book is too child-oriented?

Harold: I don't know. That's our life right now. They bring out tenderness in us. In some ways it's a lot easier to express love to the kids than it is to each other. In fact, it's almost awkward, sometimes, to express romantic affection after you've been married for a time. It's parallel to the spiritual thing. Sometimes we feel awkward sharing spiritually, and there's an awkwardness that comes in expressing ourselves romantically. This is the person you get up in the morning with and you argue with—romantic words seem out of place.

Jeanette: It is easy to walk past a kid and just grab him up in your arms and hug him and tickle him and say, "Oh, I sure am glad you're my little kid."

Harold: And yet spouses need that in the same way that the kid needs it.

Jeanette: We're so free with our emotions with the kids.

Harold: They bring out the relaxed freedom. You can wrestle them to the floor and you can be silly with a child.

Jeanette: Nuzzle their necks—all that stuff that we love. How often do I say to my kids, "Oh, I'm so glad you're my kid!" But how often do I say to you, "Oh, I'm so glad you're my husband"?

Harold: Somehow we expect that to be understood automatically. "The spouse doesn't need to be told." Yet we do! If you're not told you're loved, you really don't know it. You can't just decipher or assume that. Sure, we say it in ways other than words. But we need the words, too.

Jeanette: I love you.

Harold: Maybe it sounds trite—but I'll say it anyway, 'cause it's true.

I love you, Jeanette!

8
SEX IN DECADE TWO

All week we've been crashing through life,
flopping into bed at twelve,
exhaling like workhorses unharnessed at last.
Sex?
With the alarm set for 6:30?
With both of us sinking into the mattress?
A gentle pat,
your leg arched over mine,
a "Goodnight, Love."
That'll do
for tonight
for tomorrow night.
The young and the beautiful,
they'd look on us in amusement.
"The fires are dampened,"
they'd sadly commiserate.
"Married 12 years—
how dull!
The best is gone;
they're dead from the neck down!"

What image is less sensual
than Mom and Dad wandering around in bathrobes,
picking up kids' dirty socks,
getting ready for bed?

Alongside of that marvelous honeymoon night,
contrasted with our first year together,
yes, sex is different now.
Ten years ago, the engine was always steamed,
and it took very little to activate it.
Now, the steam must be built up,
in a thousand different ways.
But isn't that the plan?
Isn't that the challenge?
To be forced to show love all day—
or to miss out on the best sex of our lives?
In so many ways, the best is now!
Our loving is such a mixture,
intertwined with our kissable kids
and all the miles we've ridden together.
Oh, less frequent maybe.
With heavy roles to play as parents and providers,
we're not to simply gratify ourselves.
We're to open our flawed persons to each other,
to help and complement,
not demand performance
sexual or otherwise,
but to pitch in and help,
to listen to you when you can't cope
or feel trapped by demands.
That's the real foreplay!
All this is sexual,
all this is part of our union,
even when it doesn't lead to the sensual.

My duty is to love you.
My duty includes all the tedious things.
But drab duty turns into joy!
To love you
is to make things easier for you,
to give you my time,
to praise you,

to share the loads.
All this is the stuff of life,
the stuff of obedience to God,
the stuff of delight!

And now, we've started
our special weekend together.
These three days in Chicago,
just the two of us,
are worth the hotel bills and food checks.
Yes, sex is different now,
and better, in its own ways.
Now, we are not automatically turned on,
as if we were newlyweds.
No matter how many books we might read
on positions and variations
and standing on your head,
it's still the same sexuality.
But it's better than ever,
because it's with you
because it's a thing of joy that says
even though we've been angry last week
or tired
or disjointed and tense
or feeling like failures,
we go somewhere, the two of us,
to say, "I love you,"
verbally, physically;
to share our most intimate fantasies
and touch the core of each other.

We've seen prostitutes outside our hotel,
out in the Chicago streets.
What's wrong with their selling their bodies?
We are here in our hotel room
and they lead men to theirs.
What's the difference?

It is not the pleasure that's wrong,
but what they rob themselves of—
a God-blessed sexuality which includes
the playfulness in the bed
growing out of total intimacy;
the clean joy of love
that mixes with pleasure.
All their orgies and bed-hopping
without the intimacy of persons under God—
how empty,
how ultimately boring,
how tragic for man and woman
when God designed so much more!

But cannot marriage produce its own emptiness,
an airless corridor of aseptic relationships?
The prostitutes practice the gymnastics of sex.
The free-and-easy give moments of pleasure.
But are we ready for the hard work of sex—
the labors of love,
concern for each other
that makes our love more than carnal pleasure?
If we retreat into self,
our sex is little better than lustful orgies.
But if we assume the "yoke" of sharing the pains,
and each other's burdens,
our love will be unique,
wrapped up ultimately with childbearing,
and child rearing, and being a "family,"
enriching and satisfying in a new way each year,
when we're forty, fifty, sixty. . . .

SEX IN DECADE TWO

How beautiful your sandaled feet, O prince's daughter! Your graceful legs are like jewels, the work of a craftsman's hands. Your navel is a rounded goblet that never lacks blended wine. Your waist is a mound of wheat encircled by lilies. Your breasts are like two fawns, twins of a gazelle. Your neck is like an ivory tower. Your eyes are the pools of Heshbon by the gate of Bath Rabbim. Your nose is like the tower of Lebanon looking toward Damascus. Your head crowns you like Mount Carmel. Your hair is like royal tapestry; the king is held captive by its tresses.

How beautiful you are and how pleasing, O love, with your delights! Your stature is like that of the palm, and your breasts like clusters of fruit. I said, "I will climb the palm tree; I will take hold of its fruit." May your breasts be like the clusters of the vine, the fragrance of your breath like apples, and your mouth like the best wine.
—Song of Songs 7:1-9

I am a wall, and my breasts are like towers. Thus I have become in his eyes like one bringing contentment.
—Song of Songs 8:10

"Where is your wife, Sarah?" they asked him. "There, in the tent," he said. Then the Lord said, "I will surely return to you about this time next year, and Sarah your wife will have a son."

Now Sarah was listening at the entrance to the tent, which was behind him. Abraham and Sarah were already old and well-advanced in years, and Sarah was past the age of childbearing. So Sarah laughed to herself as she thought, "After I am worn out and my master is old, will I now have this pleasure?"

Then the Lord said to Abraham, "Why did Sarah laugh and say, 'Will I really have a child, now that I am old?' Is anything too hard for the Lord? I will return to you at the appointed time next year and Sarah will have a son." Sarah was afraid, so she lied and said, "I did not laugh." But he said, "Yes, you did laugh."

Now the Lord was gracious to Sarah as He had said, and the Lord did for Sarah what He had promised. Sarah became pregnant and bore a son to Abraham in his old age, at the very time God had promised him.—Genesis 18:9-15; 20:1-2

A word aptly spoken is like apples of gold in settings of silver.—Proverbs 25:11

Like clouds and wind without rain is a man who boasts of gifts he does not give.—Proverbs 25:14

9

THE AWESOME YOU

The bumper sticker
on sale in Walt's Supermarket
audaciously confronted me—
VERY IMPORTANT PERSON: PASS WITH AWE.

It was grouped with other slogans
flippant or crude,
the sort of bumper message
that matches adolescent imperiousness:
a boy drawing on a cigarette like Humphrey Bogart
while flooring the gas pedal.
The slogan writer surely viewed his words
as absurdist humor,
never noticing he was providing
such fine theology for the supermarket.

It made me think of you, Jeanette.
I read, talk, eat, sleep
with an eternal person,
someone God himself weeps over,
delights in, yearns for.

It made me remember C.S. Lewis' words:
   It is a serious thing
   to live in a society of possible gods and goddesses,

to remember that
the dullest and most uninteresting person you talk to
may one day be a creature which,
if you saw it now,
you would be strongly tempted to worship,
or else a horror and a corruption. . . .

All day long we are,
in some degree,
helping each other to one or another
of these destinations . . .
it is immortals whom we joke with,
work with,
marry, snub and exploit—
immortal horrors, or everlasting splendours.*

Which, Jeanette, am I helping you to become?
We talk about how much we daily mold our children—
how they believe about themselves,
what we communicate to them.

In the same way, my attitudes toward you,
help make you what you'll become;
they mold your perceptions of yourself.

I shape you by my grunts or smiles,
my complaints or laughter,
the messages I send your way in an evening.
Are you love or pest?
Person or irritant?
Do I lift you toward God
or drag you toward hell?
After a lifetime of marriage,
you will be—in a thousand ways—

*"The Weight of Glory," Wm. B. Eerdmans, p. 15

my creation
and I yours.
We shape each other.
We stunt growth
or free it to reach toward our Creator.

I still regret that time
I returned from a weekend out East.
You had cared for the kids
and worked very, very hard on a project you hate:
organizing the basement.
You had bitten the bullet,
cleaned and categorized,
while hovering over three lively kids
during a long, long weekend.
Then I came home Sunday,
from a tiring but pleasant adult setting,
and when you showed me
all you had done,
I said it was fine,
but we needed shelves,
and a more complete organizational plan,
and that I was very tired myself.

I had an opportunity to enrich you,
to make your weekend complete and end well,
but my response showed I didn't empathize.
I made you miserable and resentful,
and created bad days for both of us.

A word of praise, of kindness,
or loving but tactful concern,
at other times perhaps godly rebuke—
all can help you grow in God.

Do I love you enough
to accept your imperfections

as well as all your assets?
Are we children playing house,
or are we mature lovers,
understanding the hard edges of life,
helping each other face the new problems,
the new frustrations that rise as life changes?

I, like you, am not a rock,
but flesh and emotions.
Sometimes I want to say to you,
"Do not attack me!"
You see me as so strong,
but I am not;
I am vulnerable,
and though I clench teeth and move on,
with defensive reactions to cover my hurt,
verbal blows cut and bruise.
Yet when I attack you,
I seldom think of how easily hurt you are.
"Bear one another's burdens," Scripture says.
Do I?

An unkind word,
just one,
is like a bullet
which pierces flesh
and rips through vital organs.

But a loving word
is like a raindrop
which pleasantly touches the flesh.

What are the loving words and touches
which will make you
a creature of God's love
and righteousness

years and years from now?
What are the hard truths
we must face together?
How can we truly love?

A word of praise
at a straightened basement,
an ungrudging, patient nod
at a late arrival,
an insight offered
when temptation overpowers,
how large the challenge
in a thousand little things.

Every day I need signs from you, Lover—
that you're my friend,
that we mean much to each other,
that there's something you like about me
right now.
I need the small gesture
a touch
one word
because love doesn't take care of itself.
And nothing kills it like apathy
silence
grunting through the tasks
and forgetting our persons.

Only as we share
are we part of the great adventure
of seeing each other grow.

And as we grow
in insight, perception, skills,
we must help each other grow toward God.
For in our sophistication,

we can so easily worship our own creations,
our creature comforts,
or each other.

By sharing
we can merge
all we learn about child-rearing,
and following God according to the Bible,
and Lewis, Thielicke, Tournier,
into our own hours together,
in sandy bathrooms
and messy basements
and barged-into bedrooms.
You're becoming an incredible creature, you know,
because He is in you.
Let us give Him a free hand
in these creatures He is fashioning.

THE AWESOME YOU

For You created my inmost being; You knit me together in my mother's womb. I praise You because I am fearfully and wonderfully made; Your works are wonderful, I know that full well. My frame was not hidden from You when I was made in the secret place. When I was woven together in the depths of the earth, Your eyes saw my unformed body. All the days ordained for me were written in Your book before one of them came to be.

How precious to me are Your thoughts, O God! How vast is the sum of them! Were I to count them, they would outnumber the grains of sand. When I awake, I am still with you.——Psalm 139:13-18

For we are God's workmanship, created in Christ Jesus to do good works, which God prepared in advance for us to do.——Ephesians 2:10

If you have any encouragement from being united with Christ, if any comfort from His love, if any fellowship with the Spirit, if any tenderness and compassion, then make my joy complete by being like-minded, having the same love, being one in spirit and purpose. Do nothing out of selfish ambition or vain conceit, but in humility consider others better than yourselves. Each of you should look not only to your own interests, but also to the interests of others.——Philippians 2:1-4

Love must be sincere. Hate what is evil; cling to what is good. Be devoted to one another in brotherly love. Honor one another above yourselves.——Romans 12:9-10

10
LET'S KEEP OUR LOVE ALIVE

Hey, Lover!
Say, Jeanette!
Let's keep our love alive!
Feed it.
Keep it warm and friendly,
fun to feel
and a joy to touch.

Say, Lover!
Let's spin around,
and lose our gravity,
shuck our gravity,
spin high and laughing.
I feel like whirling you around,
laughing silly, holding hands,
leaping up side by side,
open to each other,
open like two kids chasing the moon.
Let's be kids today!
Why not?
I'm in a childish mood.
Be "as little children"
with the masks dropped
and the smiles large.

Let's grab a piece of childhood;
let's feed our love some joy!

Say, Lover!
What should we feed our love?
Ordinary things,
in our ordinary lives,
they'll do us very nicely,
if they're packaged by our love.

Let's feed our hungry love.
How about popcorn in the park,
animal crackers at dawn?
Feed it peanut butter sandwiches,
asparagus and peas.
Something simple,
something green or yellow or blue—
anything will feed our love,
if we hand it to each other.

Let's feed our love,
simple things—
a couple of chairs,
a glass of milk,
a napkin to share the edges of—
that's all we need.

Let's find the joy
that's promised us,
a child's joy,
released from guilt, and fears.

Where?
How can we be like children?
Obey the Lord!
That's the way to joy.

Is that sermonic?
Tedious?
No, the opposite—the door to freedom.
We've always known it.

Like the song:
"Love and marriage,
love and marriage,
go together like a horse and carriage."
It's quite the same:
"Joy and obeying,
joy and obeying,
go together. . . ."

Hey!
Throw your arms wide to the wind,
wide to the Spirit,
wide to our love.
We can't have one
without the other!
We can't know joy
without the Lord!

Say, let's feed our love
a thousand meals of soup and bread,
a thousand plates and cups and spoons,
in our ordinary
everyday
up-in-the-morning
wash-your-face
check-the-kids type of days.
Let's feed our love
with love and joy and peace
and patience too, and gentle words
and goodness, yes,
and self-control.

Let's feed our love,
my wife,
feed it kisses
and sprigs of wild flowers,
feed it touches on face
on cheek
on shoulder,
feed it words
a thousand words
like "I'm sorry"
"Please touch me"
"I missed you"
"Help me, huh?"
"Betcha can't catch me!"

Hey! Say,
let's feed our love.
Stuff it with the simple things—
gratitude and giving,
caring when we're crabby,
feed it pickles for zing
and apples and bread.
Who cares?
Give it cozy things,
with a loving hand,
but never spiders tossed down backs,
or creepy crawly things,
or rocks and bricks.

Say, Lover,
fly me to the moon
with that impish look of yours.
Let's talk again of when
a monkey sat on my head,
in the State of California;
or the day you stood up tall

as the convertible bounced along,
or the day you pulled me onto a bed
of soft pine needles on a lonely mountain.
Say! Let's be kids again!

But, wait!
This kid-like thing
is more like you than me!
You're the free spirit!
Are you infecting me,
the curmudgeonly carthorse?
Are you infusing me with your enthusiasms?
Say!
I hope so.

It's time we laughed!
After all, who should be laughing?
We, the forgiven!
We, the redeemed!
Who should be filled with joy?
We who have a million years,
to laugh and worship,
to leap for joy.
Who should delight
in being seduced by his wife,
but a person who knows
the One who created all this—
man and woman,
touch and tingle,
sexual glances and stirring.
He made them all.
Hey, Lover,
let's feed our love,
with laughing hi-jinks under covers!
Who made this silly laughter in a bed?
Who put Solomon's Song in His book?
Who made our marvelous bodies,

and your impish look,
your coy wink?

Hey! Say, Lover,
let's feed our love,
with all the simple things,
the sexy things,
the childlike things,
all the joyous, earthy gifts
our Creator gave us,
with His blessing,
and His laughter in our ears.

LETS KEEP OUR LOVE ALIVE

Let him kiss me with the kisses of his mouth—for your love is more delightful than wine.—Song of Songs 1:2

When the Lord brought back the captives to Zion, we were like men who dreamed. Our mouths were filled with laughter, our tongues with songs of joy. Then it was said among the nations, "The Lord has done great things for them." The Lord has done great things for us, and we are filled with joy.—Psalm 126:1-3

Praise the Lord. Praise God in His sanctuary; praise Him in His mighty heavens. Praise Him for His acts of power; praise Him for His surpassing greatness. Praise Him with the sounding of the trumpet, praise Him with the harp and lyre, praise Him with tambourine and dancing, praise Him with the strings and flute, praise Him with the clash of cymbals, praise Him with resounding cymbals. Let everything that has breath praise the Lord. Praise the Lord. —Psalm 150

Be imitators of God, therefore, as dearly loved children and live a life of love, just as Christ loved us and gave Himself up for us as a fragrant offering and sacrifice to God.—Ephesians 5:1-2

A happy heart makes the face cheerful, but heartache crushes the spirit.—Proverbs 15:13

Rejoice in the Lord always. I will say it again: Rejoice! Let your gentleness be evident to all. The Lord is near.

Do not be anxious about anything, but in everything, by prayer and petition, with thanksgiving, present your request to God. And the peace of God, which transcends all understanding, will guard your hearts and your minds in Christ Jesus.

Finally, brothers, whatever is true, whatever is noble, whatever is right, whatever is pure, whatever is lovely, whatever is admirable—if anything is excellent or praiseworthy—think about such things.—Philippians 4:4-8

11
SPIRITUAL GIANTS, SPIRITUAL BABES

"Love
does not consist in gazing at each other,
but in looking together in the same direction."

St. Exupery* said it.
But how are we to look together,
when we are different as hawk and bluebird,
robin and gull?

In some ways
we match Jane and Michael
but in reverse.
She's more like me, and Michael's more like you.
Jane's emotional electricity
charged their living room last night
as the four of us grappled
with her intensity about God,
and his lukewarm attitudes.
We could tell he felt threatened
as they shared the problem.
She makes him miserable
with her insistence that he too
experience a rich spiritual life,

---

*Author of "The Little Prince"

as she is these days,
and that he not revel in his consultant work,
replacing God with success.
Is she right?
He's a free spirit,
a "people person."
Maybe he's not lukewarm spiritually.
Maybe he just doesn't get all that intense.
He'll never have night visions
or agonizing hours on his knees.

Though both Michael and Jane fail God,
Michael's failures loom larger,
more visible.
Yet maybe she is right.
Maybe his admitting his need
for more commitment to Christ
and yet ever failing
is the sort of Pharisaism
that kills the spirit,
the sort of easy believism
that lets the world move on toward hell.

Why doesn't Michael care as much as Jane does?
Does God work differently in him?
Does Michael have a smaller "gift of faith?"
Or in his "simple" faith
does he trust God just as much?

Their conflict tears at the roots
of their committed marriage.
Her advice and concern,
instead of healing
or bringing them the oneness she wants,
injects a foreign agent.
Yet I cannot fault her spirit.
Perhaps it's the man-wife barrier.

Most of us would rather take
advice from a stranger than a spouse.
There's something about a spouse
trying to improve the mate
which raises the hackles.

Is this a reason that
the more Jane says
"Shape up, pray more,
live what you preach,
commit yourself fully,"
the more he resents the attack
and retreats to his work?
Feeling vaguely ambivalent
that maybe she's right,
but maybe she's wrong about him?
Is this what Jesus meant
when he said he'd bring
a sword between loved ones?
A spiritual battle for total allegiance?
Or is it Satan sneaking in,
blinding them both
to the diversity of personalities?
Whichever it is,
they seem on a spiritually destructive course,
even though both are very aware Christians,
aware of the dynamics they stand waist-deep in,
yet struggling to find
the way out.
There are no simple spiritual answers
when you hit real people like this
who struggle in the arena . . . .

There's an obvious danger, though.
So many couples
construct an unwieldly balance
of spiritual giant

wedded to spiritual babe.
In some ways,
our marriage started out like that.
My spiritual intensity was the hallmark.
I was the mentor,
the driving force you were to emulate.
Yet you stood on your own turf,
and now,
after nearly a dozen years together,
who is to say who serves God better?
You're the one who dials Christian FM,
leads in Bible School, Sunday School,
teaches Christian songs to our kids.
You care about people,
and you reach out in Jesus' name.

Yet you want more communion with God,
more time in prayer,
more time listening to Him.
Is this a model
imposed on us by other Christians?
Or Scripture's clear command?

And I?
I long for more "childlike" faith,
that natural peace and acceptance
which is part of your temperament.

Strange.
We complement each other
and each of us helps the other.
But these differences,
both in our marriage
and in Jane and Michael's marriage,
and in so many others
creates heat, seldom love,
and sets one spouse against the other.

Lukewarmness is sin. True.
But clearly, it is equally true
Satan uses everything he can
to wedge lovers apart—
our diverse spiritual gifts,
our unique, conflicting personalities.
He uses anything to rend the fabric,
instead of allowing the diversity
to enrich us with color and depth.

"Everything you do is important,"
you said with gentle sarcasm not long ago,
"but what I do is frivolous.
Welcome Wagon is frivolous.
Decorating the house is a waste of time—
we could 'make do,'
who needs all this fuss and expense?
What I do doesn't count—
but you're the good guy;
I waste my time and money,
but you. . ."

You said it in a moment of frustration.
Yet there was truth there;
this had been grinding on you.
We do have conflicting ideas,
especially about time and money.
But if you feel this way
I must be laying it on you somehow.
I'll have to admit it, yes,
I feel I do concentrate on the "oughts,"
the necessities,
and you start with the icing
instead of the cake.
I worry about standing before God,
and giving account of my use of money,
yet I can't say

when it comes to actions
that I am more generous than you.

If you feel I judge you,
we can't let that ride beneath the surface
eating away at our love,
the way the "little foxes" do
with Jane and Michael.

Do I feel your work is frivolous?
You know I don't
but it's easy for me to imply that,
when we haven't discussed priorities,
and agreed to them together,
and pressures start to build in us both.
It's easy for me to use a spiritual club,
that my priority choices
are more valid than yours.
There are so many ways
a spiritual club can be used.
In the hands of a wife,
it can be even more deadly,
for it has an added spike:
the husband is failing in his responsibility
as "spiritual leader of the home."
What guilt wives can generate,
as that particular spike
on the edge of the knobby club
is swung toward his head as he watches TV.
How easily a husband
is transformed into a second-class human,
having abdicated his true role,
and now the wife must take up her cross,
because he has failed.

Satan has an awesome bag of tricks
and he'll use whatever works,

one on us,
another on Jane and Michael.
And we can never precisely figure out
what his game plan is.

It's a mystery,
for it's true the husband may not be as "spiritual,"
and if one doesn't give a rip
about prayer, or Bible, or Christians,
he's spiritually stagnant.
But how did he get that way?
And how much
is jockeying for power in the marriage?

Evil finds so many ways,
to penetrate,
to throw off balance,
to start two people into a pattern
that sets them against each other
and through that, eventually against God too,
even though one spouse
is thoroughly absorbed in church.

I find it true, more each time it happens,
that I cannot be right with God
when I'm not right with you.

When we came back
from that wonderful, loving vacation,
it seemed incredible to me
that we could have a spat,
one day—just one day—later.
Now we can both
reconstruct the causes,
and it was probably inevitable.
Our smiles about it today
smooth it all,

but during that evening,
I was not only estranged from you
but also estranged from God
And it seems to me
that if the evil powers
can just build dynamics to wedge us apart,
Satan will erect, with the same bricks,
walls that split us from God,
from our children,
from those who need us.

We have always found it very difficult
to regularly pray together.
We felt almost relieved to learn
that Paul Tournier and his wife
simply couldn't pray together at first.
Yet eventually, it led them
to marvelous enrichment.

The spiritual sharing we have done,
whether Bible study or prayer,
starts hard
because we are so different,
but the rewards are there.
Most things with big rewards
take large effort.
Why do we feel
that spiritual efforts should be easy?
We are in spiritual warfare.
If Satan is not out to get us,
our own lusts and weaknesses can.
We need each other
spiritually,
for God put us together
to worship and commune with Him,
to pray for each other—
including our spiritual vitality.

Yes, it's hard,
hard as swallowing vinegar sometimes,
to take a mate's advice,
let alone reproof.
To admit a weakness.
To not worry about losing turf
in the marriage power game.
In these years,
have we matured enough,
stabilized enough,
to realize it's our mate who loves us
who wants the best for us?

SPIRITUAL GIANTS, SPIRITUAL BABES

Blessed are those who hunger and thirst for righteousness, for they will be filled.—Matthew 5:6

As the deer pants for streams of water, so my soul pants for You, O God. My soul thirsts for God, for the living God. When can I go and meet with God? My tears have been my food day and night, while men say to me all day long, "Where is your God?" These things I remember as I pour out my soul: how I used to go with the multitude, leading the procession to the house of God, with shouts of joy and thanksgiving among the festive throng.

Why are you downcast, O my soul? Why so disturbed within me? Put your hope in God, for I will yet praise Him, my Saviour and my God.

My soul is downcast within me; therefore I will remember You from the land of Jordan, the heights of Hermon—from Mount Mizar. Deep calls to deep in the roar of your waterfalls; all your waves and breakers have swept over me.

By day the Lord directs His love, at night His song is with me—a prayer to the God of my life.

I say to God my Rock, "Why have You forgotten me? Why must I go about mourning, oppressed by the enemy?" My bones suffer mortal agony as my foes taunt me, saying to me all day long, "Where is your God?"

Why are you downcast, O my soul? Why so disturbed within me? Put your hope in God, for I will yet praise Him, my Saviour and my God.—Psalm 42

O God, You are my God, earnestly I seek You; my soul

thirsts for You, my body longs for You, in a dry and weary land where there is no water.

I have seen You in the sanctuary and beheld Your power and Your glory. Because Your love is better than life, my lips will glorify You. I will praise You as long as I live, and in Your name I will lift up my hands. My soul will be satisfied as with the richest of foods; with singing lips my mouth will praise You.

On my bed I remember You; I think of You through the watches of the night. Because You are my help, I sing in the shadow of Your wings. I stay close to You; Your right hand upholds me.—Psalm 63:1-8

May the God of hope fill you with all joy and peace as you trust in Him, so that you may overflow with hope by the power of the Holy Spirit.—Romans 15:13

For this reason I kneel before the Father, from whom His whole family in heaven and on earth derives its name. I pray that out of His glorious riches He may strengthen you with power through His Spirit in your inner being, so that Christ may dwell in your hearts through faith. And I pray that you, being rooted and established in love, may have power, together with all the saints, to grasp how wide and how long and high and deep is the love of Christ, and to know this love that surpasses knowledge—that you may be filled to the measure of all the fullness of God.
—Ephesians 3:14-19

Finally, be strong in the Lord and in His mighty power. Put on the full armor of God so that you can take your stand against the devil's schemes. For our struggle is not against flesh and blood, but against rulers, against the authorities, against the powers of this dark world and against the spiritual forces of evil in the heavenly realms.
—Ephesians 6:10-12

12
BEYOND COMMUNI-CATION

Your side:

As you step into the house,
fresh from your 6 a.m. swim at the "Y,"
you nearly trip over the misplaced rug.
Another irritant from the children!
You then learn a wooden chair was left outside.
Naturally, it rained last night.
"Can it be fixed?" Michelle asks.
"I suppose it can," you reply,
"if I carry it to the furniture store,
then go look for special polish,
and run all over town with it!"
Just one more problem,
added to the interminable list:
haircuts for both boys,
groceries,
music lesson (pick up, drop off),
piles of wash,
the church committee,
and vacation in just three days,
with your husband untanned and uncooperative.
"Going to the beach with us today?" you ask.
"So you can get your tan started?"

My objections nettle you,
and you react with considerable heat:
"So you'll be the spoilsport
three weeks from now!
You won't stay out in the boat,
since your nose and legs will get burned.
You've got to get some sun now!
But no,
We'll be at that lakeside condo
for a whole week of water fun
and you'll be looking for shade,
like a grumpy mole.
I've been getting a tan
so we can have fun with our friends,
but you'll kill the fun.
You don't care about your body.
We women keep our bodies trim and tanned
for you men.
But you don't care what you look like for me."

I argue that tan is a recent cultural bias,
that white is beautiful,
but you don't buy it—
you know I put low priority on my appearance.

You pause and look at yesterday's picnic chaos
still spread through the kitchen.
"And now you go off to a neat office,
where everyone helps keep it tidy,
instead of home,
where kids all do their share
toward messing it up!
There's just too much to do,"
I suggest you could skip the beach,
but you say summer's almost over,
the kids love the beach.

"What's life supposed to be,
just work, work, work?"

My side:

"Well, yes," my mind responds,
"that's precisely what life is,"
but I do not voice it.
You are down emotionally
and I must understand,
not combat.

I despise beaches.
We went to one on the weekend,
which was more than enough.
What an absurdity—
bodies smeared with unpleasant oils,
stretched on the itchy sand among biting bugs,
cooking like skinned meat under a fire.
People choose such masochism?
For what?
For beautiful skin?
Not many years ago,
women would do anything to get no sun,
to be "white and lovely."
Why must I fit into your designs
for my vacation?
"Everyone will be out under the sun—
you'll be the party-pooper."
Too bad! It's my vacation too,
and I'd rather read "War and Peace," thank you,
in the air conditioning,
not out on the sizzling sand.
I want to play tennis,
    and swim,
    and hike—in the shade!

Your pressures? I have a few—
I'm hit from ten directions at the office,
then five more at home.
And, yes, my office is organized,
partly because I set priorities,
which doesn't mean doing everything in sequence,
but not doing
about 70 percent of the "good ideas."
Less is more!
That could work at home too.

Our side:

Tournier says lack of complete frankness
is the most frequent marriage problem.
Well, we're pretty frank.
We open up and share it all.
But then what?
"Love is patient and kind."
We should sacrifice for each other.
Yet I'm still not going to the beach today.
I really don't believe
my constant giving in
would help either of us—
nor would your giving it to me.
How do we submit to each other
Yet honestly express our feelings?
How can we not be doormats,
yet show empathy?

I admit I seldom do something
strictly because I love you.
There's usually some benefit to me.
Am I here to serve you?
Really?
And you to serve me?
Those sentiments look wonderful

on wedding cards
and books with photos of lovers in wheatfields.
But how do they work in our kitchen?

So often, what's important to you
is not important to me,
and vice versa.
It's the natural trap
of two persons living together.

It seems to me
that marriage is like a slippery hill,
with Jack and Jill on opposite sides,
trying to pull themselves up to the top.
With no effort, we slide to the bottom,
miles away from each other.
If our hands are not linked,
our arms encircling the hill,
we have no leverage,
no way to pull up.
No, love doesn't take care of itself,
and without linked hands,
we crash to the bottom.

Can I confront my own selfishness
in specifics
like beaches?
Can I take your complaints
not as an attack on me,
but as a statement of how you feel?
Can I peer deeply into your soul—
even deeper than the words you say—
and love the core of you?
How can we care about
our deepest drives and doubts and hurts?

The fact is, we have both heard my angst so often

it's become a tired record—
even to me.
A few weeks ago we sat watching "Annie Hall,"
and Woody Allen admits to her,
if there's a starving person somewhere,
anywhere on earth,
it ruins his evening.
And it's so funny in context
that you laugh
laugh heartily, knowingly.
You look over at me,
for I had said literally and exactly the same thing
over a seafood dinner just hours before—
only, no one laughed, of course,
and even I had been bored by my own comment,
the same old angst,
the same old doubts.
So there I was,
a Woody Allen without the humor.
(What an unpalatable condition!)
Am I a "tortured intellectual"?
(How posturing? How accurate? Such thin gruel for life?)
You've heard it all before—
those anguished thoughts of mine,
as well as the spiritual triumphs.
All our married life
we've spoken of my going to spiritual peaks,
but also low valleys,
while you accept, believe,
live on an even keel.

So you see into my soul.
But do you?
Or can we but touch the surface
of our deepest persons?
Can we really "read" the other
from words and gestures and sighs?

Or do our readings add up
to just a first-grade primer?
I wish, I really wish,
I could climb behind your eyes,
and feel and see and smell and taste
as you do.

I wrote this once,
on a day I must have felt very vulnerable:
"Don't argue with me,
to show me I'm wrong.
I feel wrong and unworthy most of the time."
I am not Ulysses.
We need to see each other,
and listen,
and see ourselves—

"Lord, search me,
and know my heart;
try me, and know my thoughts,
and see if there be any wicked way in me,
and lead me in the paths of righteousness."

Only God can give
both insights and love
that reverse the action-reaction,
the self-centered viewpoint,
the seeing through only my glasses.
Only He can give the balance,
between my being a doormat
or a sledgehammer.

This evening we are sitting at Big Boy,
eating fish and chips with the children.
You look,
I must admit,
very cute with your light tan.

You look at me with your little-girl smile,
and say, "It's so easy to talk about conflict,
and how to resolve it—
but when you're in it! . . ."

I smile back.
"I think you were just venting this morning," I say.
"You hit all those pressures,
you were tired."

"Yes," you agree,
and you look at me warmly,
and you say, very lovingly,
"Thank you for coming back this morning,
and for kissing me before you left.
That said to me
that you knew I was just upset,
That you weren't going to be mad at me all day.
That really helped me this morning—
kept me from having a rotten day."

Amazing.
I had forgotten
that I'd come back from the car
and given you a little kiss and a pat.
The little actions do help.
Even if I wasn't feeling 100 percent loving,
it was right to reach out,
to act, despite my own building resentments.

Your words and your eyes,
as you thank me,
buoy my emotions
and make me want to sit with you
alone for awhile,
under an apple tree or by a beach,

and find out more about this woman I married,
who can take a very small gift from her husband
and return it
enlarged and melodious.

BEYOND COMMUNICATION

Do everything without complaining or arguing, so that you may become blameless and pure, children of God without fault in a crooked and depraved generation, in which you shine like stars in the universe. . . .—Philippians 2:14-15

Reckless words pierce like a sword, but the tongue of the wise brings healing.—Proverbs 12:18

He who listens to a life-giving rebuke will be at home among the wise. The fear of the Lord teaches a man wisdom, and humility comes before honor.—Proverbs 15:31, 33

Like a city whose walls are broken down is a man who lacks self-control.—Proverbs 25:28

A fool finds no pleasure in understanding but delights in airing his own opinions. He who answers before listening —that is his folly and his shame.—Proverbs 18:2, 13

An honest answer is like a kiss on the lips.—Proverbs 24:26

The entire Law is summed up in a single command: "Love your neighbor as yourself." If you keep on biting and devouring each other, watch out or you will be destroyed by each other.

So I say, live by the Spirit, and you will not gratify the desires of the sinful nature.—Galatians 5:14-16

Do not repay anyone evil for evil. Be careful to do what is right in the eyes of everybody. If it is possible, as far as it depends on you, live at peace with everyone.—Romans 12:17-18

If a man pays back evil for good, evil will never leave his house. Starting a quarrel is like breaching a dam; so drop the matter before a dispute breaks out.—Proverbs 17:13-14

As a north wind brings rain, so a sly tongue brings angry looks. Better to live on a corner of the roof than share a house with a quarrelsome wife.—Proverbs 25:23-24

We who are strong ought to bear with the failings of the weak and not to please ourselves. Each of us should please his neighbor for his good, to build him up. For even Christ did not please Himself but, as it is written: "The insults of those who insult you have fallen on Me." For everything that was written in the past was written to teach us, so that through endurance and the encouragement of the Scriptures we might have hope.

May the God who gives endurance and encouragement give you a spirit of unity among yourselves as you follow Christ Jesus, so that with one heart and mouth you may glorify the God and Father of our Lord Jesus Christ.

Accept one another, then, just as Christ accepted you, in order to bring praise to God.—Romans 15:1-7

Since we live by the Spirit, let us keep in step with the Spirit. Let us not become conceited, provoking and envying each other.—Galatians 5:25-26

13
A MAN LOOKS AT HIS FAMILY

I enter our darkened home,
after writing in a restaurant for hours.
It's 1 a.m.
My footsteps waken no one.
You and the children sleep in your rooms,
trusting.

I step in to check little Greg.
Beside his crib
a big panda stares from a poster.
Greg lies tangled in his blanket,
blond hair against the sheets,
his midriff bare between tops and bottoms.

We almost didn't have Gregory.
One boy, one girl,
that was enough,
a matched pair, ecologically correct.
But one night, I thought,
if there were a fire,
what do I care about saving?
Jeanette, Michelle, and Todd.
Nothing else.
Manuscripts. Money. Paintings.
Nothing mattered.

If two children meant so much,
why not just one more?

Welcome, Greg!

Just hours ago,
I was tossing Gregory into the air,
amazed at his lightness.
"What a fun toy I have here!"
I said loudly,
"Much better than a teddy bear.
How much does this giggle-toy cost, Todd?
Ten dollars?"
And Todd, losing his sibling rivalry,
joined right in,
"Yes, ten dollars.
What a great toy!
Buy him!"
And then, after the tenth bounce,
Todd observed, "Isn't he cute!"

But I also scolded Greg today,
and he ran off, insulted.
Ten minutes later,
he appeared at the head of the stairs.
"I'll be your friend, Greg,
if you'll be mine."
He wanted an apology, not this.
He put on his bashful look,
ambivalent,
and finally walked past me to his toys.
But five minutes later,
his usual good spirits bubbled up.

Gregory: squealing delight;
           quietly playing;
           saying "I love you."

But he can also say
"I hate you,"
not knowing its meaning,
but simply expressing irritation.
It's scary.
He's like a little blank tape
into which we can feed good or bad
which will then repeat
in endless variations throughout his life.
But this loving child
makes me think of you, Jeanette,
for you fill him with the good,
and he is your happy product,
secure here in his little bed,
knowing a call will bring you running,
hugging, soothing.

I cross over and look down at Todd,
beside Smithsonian airplanes on his wallpaper
which you so carefully chose,
and handmade drapes to match.
Six now, first grade,
so loving and enthusiastic,
I almost forget the small unpleasantries.
How he needs us these days,
reaching up with his arms,
wanting to go with us
for a walk or a ride or a swim.
Remember, Jeanette, a couple years ago,
when we'd left him a few days
with his Grandma and Grandpa on the farm?
Grandpa saw him standing by the barn,
looking as if he needed something.
Todd looked very serious.
Grandpa asked what was the matter.
Todd mumbled something,
stamping his feet for exclamation.

"What did you say?" Grandpa asked.
"I said, 'I need a friend!' "
"Oh," Grandpa responded.
Then he asked,
"What kind of friend?"
Todd said nothing,
but he raised his arm,
and he pointed his finger directly at Grandpa.

He has friends, in us.
He's the fruit of our love—
how utterly vital this boy
who lifts our hearts every day
when he feeds his fish,
or hammers together another airplane,
or marches to music.
How vital this boy find us still in love,
his parents, his friends,
not dwelling on our differences,
our grievances,
but loving each other so much that
our love spills out all over him.

I enter Michelle's room
with her white, frilly, canopy bed,
a Narnia book three inches from her cheek.
Each year she lives with us
she becomes far more precious than before.
I love to listen to her tell me about boys,
or teachers,
or "Little House on the Prairie,"
or read to her McDonald's fairy tales,
or watch her play with Greg
like a hovering mother.
Nine years now.
She's half raised,
and I want to stop the clock

to keep her here forever.
Dads never cry at weddings
but maybe I will anyway.
Michelle's been a mixture of ice cream and pickles
but mostly ice cream
the very best ice cream,
wonderful to us,
even meeting needs in us
we didn't realize she could touch.

I still think of that evening
when I had a virus.
Michelle was two and a half,
and listened to her ailing daddy from her crib.
It was the worst bug I'd ever had—
sharp abdominal pains
which had me rolling on the carpet,
grimacing, groaning,
seeking a position for relief.
Michelle had had much firsthand experience with
    "ouwees."
She'd fallen downstairs,
pinched her fingers,
and just then had a shot
which turned her left arm
red, swollen and very sore.

I moaned on and on
until finally
she climbed out of her crib,
Raggedy Ann in one hand,
her blanket in the other,
and stood above me, staring,
as I held my stomach.
Quietly, she reached out to me
and offered the very best remedy,
better than aspirin or heat,

her very own Raggedy Ann.
"Here, Daddy," she said softly. "Here."
Then she offered me her blanket too.

Michelle.
What a joy we share in her,
and how much she has given both of us.
Our greatest danger
is to make idols of these dear children,
to grasp them so closely
that God cannot be free
to work His unique will for each one.

Three children kissed, tucked in.
I enter our room.
It is warm.
You are sprawled on your side,
one knee up,
your nightgown disarrayed.
You are desirable,
a strange mixture of object and person,
a body that gives pleasure,
but a personality apart from my own,
vested with what Thielicke calls
"alien dignity."
If I use you
as sex object or as housewife functionary,
I violate your personhood.

Yes, you and I are
a new thing under the sun.
Two become one
shouldn't equal a predetermined "X."
Each marriage should be unique.
We are a creature in union,
made by God,
and by thousands of days together.

I look at you, my love,
sleeping in the night,
and words from Solomon's Song
describe your beauty.
The words blend
with a hundred thoughts about you.

Your remodeling the bathroom
with your own hands,
a surprise when I returned from California.

Your having over a friend
whom you were mad at;
you confessed your own attitudes
and asked forgiveness, and prayed together.

Your driving into Chicago's black South Side
to work in a Head Start program,
ignoring the danger,
risking the "do-gooder" label,
determined to help anyway.

Your telling me you hate to do dinner dishes,
your words voiced with such ferocity,
I understood a little more about our conflicts.

Your preparing stuffed pork chops,
potatoes, hot bran muffins,
fresh carrots, salad,
peach-blueberry pie and the finest coffee in town.

Your joyous embrace
on our wedding night,
your exuberance;
as both of us knew,
it was worth the waiting.

Jeanette, your body is still young,
three children later,
and still enticing.
But you think about age changing all that.
Perhaps it will.
We kid about the day,
we will sit in rockers,
with wrinkled skin and shriveled bodies,
and talk of our youth.
But, Jeanette, I'll know;
we'll both know the secret:
it will really be you,
the exuberant wedding night mistress,
wrapped in that old wrinkled skin.
It'll be you,
with that twinkle in your eyes,
and even if I can only reach over
and pat your arm,
I'll know what's hiding
under the ageing body.
"Be content
with the wife of thy youth.
Let her breasts
satisfy thee at all times."
Even when those breasts are old?
Even if a mastectomy
should remove one or both?
Yes, especially then!
We have thousands of memories
of nights like the first one,
and we grow old together,
my Love,
and you'll always be
that irrepressible 21-year-old,
coming with joy to our bed;
and you'll be the lover

who took my burdens as yours;
the lover who is more than flesh,
the person I have loved
a lifetime,
and now love the more.

I turn out the light,
and slip in beside you.
Your left leg shifts over mine,
as usual,
and I pat you gently.

A MAN LOOKS AT HIS FAMILY

The man said, "This is now bone of my bones and flesh of my flesh; she shall be called 'woman,' for she was taken out of man." For this reason a man will leave his father and mother and be united to his wife, and they will become one flesh.—Genesis 2:23-24

How beautiful you are, my darling! Oh, how beautiful! Your eyes behind your veil are doves. Your hair is like a flock of goats descending from Mount Gilead. Your teeth are like a flock of sheep just shorn, coming up from the washing. Each has its twin; not one of them is alone. Your lips are like a scarlet ribbon; your mouth is lovely. Your temples behind your veil are like the halves of a pomegranate. Your neck is like the tower of David, built with elegance; on it hang a thousand shields, all of them shields of warriors. Your two breasts are like two fawns, like twin fawns of a gazelle that browse among the lilies. Until the day breaks and the shadows flee, I will go to the mountain of myrrh and to the hill of incense. All beautiful you are, my darling; there is no flaw in you.
—Song of Songs 4:1-7

A generous man will prosper; he who refreshes others will himself be refreshed.—Proverbs 11:25

But the fruit of the Spirit is love, joy, peace, patience, kindness, goodness, faithfulness, gentleness, and self-control. Against such things there is no law.—Galatians 5:22-23

He who finds a wife finds what is good and receives favor from the Lord.—Proverbs 18:22

Wives, submit to your husbands as to the Lord. For the husband is the head of the wife as Christ is the head of the church, His body, of which He is the Saviour. Now as the church submits to Christ, so also wives should submit to their husbands in everything.

Husbands, love your wives, just as Christ loved the church and gave Himself up for her to make her holy, cleansing her by the washing with water through the Word, and to present her to Himself as a radiant church, without stain or wrinkle or any other blemish, but holy and blameless. In this same way, husbands ought to love their wives as their own bodies. He who loves his wife loves himself. After all, no one ever hated his own body, but he feeds and cares for it, just as Christ does the church— for we are members of His body. For this reason a man will leave his father and mother and be united to his wife, and the two will become one flesh. This is a profound mystery—but I am talking about Christ and the church. However, each one of you also must love his wife as he loves himself, and the wife must respect her husband. —Ephesians 5:22-23

Afterword

The Mark of the Other

Helmut Thielicke tells this story about the effect a husband and wife have on each other:

"I once knew a very old married couple who radiated a tremendous happiness. The wife especially, who was almost unable to move because of old age and illness and in whose kind old face the joys and sufferings of many years had etched a hundred runes, was filled with such gratitude for life that I was touched to the quick. Involuntarily I asked myself what could possibly be the source of this kindly person's radiance. Otherwise they were very common people and their room indicated only the most modest comfort. But suddenly I knew where it all came from, for I saw these two speaking to each other and their eyes hanging upon each other. All at once it became clear to me that this woman was dearly loved.

"It was not because she was . . . a cheerful and pleasant person that she was loved by her husband all those years. It was probably the other way around. Because she was so loved, she became the person I now saw before me."

Thielicke goes on to say that this effect can work both ways: "The other person, whom God has joined to me, is never what he is apart from me. He is not only bone of my bone; he is also boredom of my boredom and lovelessness of my lovelessness" (Helmut Thielicke, "How the World Began: Man in the First Chapter of the Bible." Fortress Press, 1961, pp. 99-100).

Thielicke holds before us stark choices. The circumstances of life and our personalities limit us; sometimes mates are caught in terrible conflicts which have no clear solutions. But the impact each of us has on our mate, whatever the circumstances, is powerful. Each of us fails. But here is a goal for all of us—to be more like that old couple Thielicke describes . . . not only to confront each other and look into each other's minds and hearts, but to also genuinely love through the daily cares and changes of life.